CRYSTAL
COMPANIONS

CRYSTAL
COMPANIONS

AN A-Z GUIDE

JESSICA LAHOUD

ROCKPOOL

A Rockpool book
PO Box 252
Summer Hill
NSW 2130
Australia

rockpoolpublishing.com
Follow us! **f** ⓞ rockpoolpublishing
Tag your images with #rockpoolpublishing

ISBN: 9781922579379

Published in 2023 by Rockpool Publishing
Copyright text © Jessica Lahoud 2023
Copyright design © Rockpool Publishing, 2023

Images from shutterstock, unsplash, pexels and Jessica Lahoud.

Design and typesetting by Sara Lindberg, Rockpool Publishing
Editing and index by Lisa Macken

A catalogue record for this
book is available from the
National Library of Australia

Printed and bound in China
10 9 8 7 6 5 4 3 2 1

CONTENTS

INTRODUCTION

I had the good fortune of being born into a crystal family. As a young girl I assumed that everybody had gems and crystals in their homes and spent their school holidays in the outback mining for precious opals, which was the norm for my parents, four sisters and me. It wasn't until I was older that I could truly appreciate the unique experiences I was sharing with my family, and it wasn't until much later still that I realised it wasn't just a nostalgic memory from my childhood but, rather, my destiny to exist in the magnificent world of crystals.

After years of travelling the world sourcing and collecting crystals of my own and then eventually opening my own crystal store, I have come to realise just how hard it can be for a beginner to find the answers they're looking for. I wrote this book in the hope it will bridge the gap between what is currently available and what is scattered across the internet and whispered between people who act as gatekeepers to the simplicity and enormous magic of crystal healing. Through my years of working in the crystal industry and owning and operating a retail crystal shop I know the questions that stump people about crystals are pretty consistent. I've put together the answers to many of those commonly asked questions so you can begin your journey with crystals with as much ease as possible. Working with crystals doesn't have to be difficult, and it doesn't have to begin with a huge collection or a lifetime's experience. Crystal healing is for everybody and should be accessible to everybody. I hope this book demystifies crystal healing for you and that you find the answers you seek in these pages.

Jessica

CHAPTER 1

HOW TO USE THIS BOOK

My goal was to put together a book that contained extensive information about crystals for anyone from beginners to more advanced crystal users and to make that information easy to follow and understand. The book covers such subjects as the importance of crystals, choosing and cleansing your crystals, crystals in your home and crystal elixirs.

As you will get the most out of your crystals if you use them in daily rituals there is a comprehensive chapter about rituals and ritual suggestions, including rituals for 12 of the crystals to begin your crystal journey. The rituals selected for those crystals were chosen on the basis of how best to connect to or utilise that crystal's metaphysical properties. Don't feel limited to those rituals, but rather see them as a starting point for you to begin to create your own rituals in your crystal journey.

Even though some of the metaphysical properties of individual crystals do cross over, every crystal has its own unique energy. When you've been working as I have with crystals for years you come to think of them as having their own personality, so the crystal descriptions have been written from each crystal's perspective so you can get to know them on a more intimate level. I hope that having the crystal spirits speak to you will help you understand your crystals and feel more connected to them, and consequently more confident in your ability to work with them effectively. The crystal A-Z has the following information about each crystal:

◈ *Element/s*: knowing the element associated with each crystal can help you to determine which method of cleansing to use and to understand more about the way the energy of the crystal interacts with your environment. For more information on these two points refer to Chapter 5 and Appendix IV.

◈ *Affirmation*: the affirmation encompasses the main message or takeaway of each crystal description. When you feel called to work with that stone use this affirmation to keep your intention focused on the energy you're cultivating.

◈ *Chakra/s*: some crystals resonate with specific energy centres in the body, or chakras. The associated chakra for each crystal has been included to help you further understand the relationship between your crystals and how they interact with your body on an energetic level.

◈ *Mohs Hardness Scale*: Mohs Hardness Scale, which measures the relative hardness of a mineral and its scratch resistance, can help you to determine the best way to care for your crystals as well as confirm their authenticity.

◈ *Pairs well with*: each crystal has a suggestion for another crystal it will pair well with so you can reflect on why they might be paired together and how the relationship between the energies of those crystals might interplay or change the outcome when you use them. You don't have to feel restricted by these pairings, and over time you will hopefully feel confident enough to make your own pairing choices to suit your unique circumstances.

◈ *Location/s*: crystals are found all over the world and new deposits of minerals are constantly being found. The countries listed in this section do not form an exhaustive list of all of the places where that stone is found but, rather, indicate the most common locations of the crystals that are sold commercially and therefore the most likely locations of the crystals you will have in your collection.

If you're looking for in-depth information I recommend reading from cover to cover, but for those who want quick answers the six appendices contain commonly asked questions and succinct reference guides.

CHAPTER 2

CRYSTALS FOR HEALING AND ENERGETIC HEALTH

Energetic health is incredibly important if you want to live a truly holistic lifestyle. By incorporating crystals into your daily routine you will give yourself little boosts throughout the day that will help you cope with the stressors of everyday life and any energetic baggage you might pick up along the way. Crystals emanate subtle energies that influence your physical, emotional and spiritual bodies. These vibrational frequencies can shift energetic blockages and allow energy to flow freely so you are not held back by them. Having the option of using mini self-care rituals with crystals is especially helpful if you don't have time to sit down and do a full body crystal grid or energy healing on a regular basis.

Sometimes after a long day at work or a social gathering you might get home feeling as though you have someone else's energy stuck to you or like a part of you is still back in the office. A short meditation with a crystal will help to settle your energy and bring you back into your centre. In this scenario there are many different crystals to choose from depending on each individual situation, but if I had to choose one I recommend selenite. Selenite, a stone of purification, is a powerful cleansing crystal that can be used to clear the stagnant or lower negative energies from a space, person or even from other crystals. Because of its powerful cleansing properties it can also dissipate brain fog and mental chatter to allow for sharp mental clarity and focus. It allows for a deeper conscious connection, empowering you to hold a higher frequency light energy. Selenite's high energy and purifying properties make it a protective stone.

IMPROVING SLEEP

When it comes to crystals to improve the length or quality of sleep there isn't a one size fits all solution, as the reasons for why you are experiencing poor or inadequate sleep can be many and varied. These are my top three recommendations for improving your sleep:

◇ Selenite's calming and purifying properties make it a great crystal to have in your bedroom to promote restful sleep. Place it on your bedside table or underneath your bed.

◇ Iolite calms an overactive mind and helps to regulate sleep patterns. Place it in your pillowcase or under your bed if you find it encourages too many dreams.

◇ Lepidolite helps to relieve stress, regulates sleeping, calms your nerves and prevents nightmares. Place it in your pillowcase for a restful slumber.

◇ If you would prefer to keep crystals out of your bedroom you can meditate with these crystals before going to bed to receive their benefits.

Selenite has calming properties that make it great for helping you sleep.

BEAUTY TOOLS

It's no secret that crystal face rollers and gua sha massage tools have taken the beauty world by storm, and when used properly they can leave you with refreshed, youthful, glowing skin. Natural crystals are cool to the touch, so on a physical level they are soothing and calming for your skin. Most of the facial massage tools on the market are carved from rose quartz or jade, and for good reason.

For centuries jade has been revered for being beneficial for overall health, harmony and balance. It strengthens and stabilises your vital life force energy, or qi. Rose quartz, the stone of love, helps to alleviate stress and brings you into a state of tranquillity and compassion.

Beyond the metaphysical properties of these two most commonly used stones, an important thing to consider is mineral safety and toxicity: not all crystals are safe for using on your face or massaging into your skin. Once you add oils or creams to the equation you run the risk of the moisture entering into the mineral and then leeching out onto your body. There isn't any regulatory body within the industry that monitors the crystals that are carved into beauty tools and sold on the market. Unfortunately, that means if people see it for sale they assume it must be safe, but many sellers are not aware of crystal toxicity. It's vital to do your own research and not trust the word of sellers when it comes to mineral toxicity. As a general rule, it's best to stick with crystals in the quartz family and jade for your beauty tools.

SUPPORTING HAPPY LIFE MOMENTS

Carnelian is the stone of courage and creativity. It helps you to step into your power and move past limiting belief patterns (impostor syndrome: I'm looking at you), and also to embrace challenges and view them as a chance to level up. Keep the momentum of a huge successful or happy moment in your life by working with carnelian, by wearing a carnelian necklace/bracelet as an amulet for positivity or through affirmations when you need a pick me up to keep that high energy momentum going.

TRY THIS RITUAL: close your eyes and hold your carnelian over your belly. Take a few deep breaths and go inwards, visualising yourself surrounded by a warm orange light. When you feel at ease, with each new breath repeat either out loud or to yourself:

I am safe.
I am confident.
I am creative.
I feel empowered.
I am strong.
I feel valued.
I am grounded.
I deserve pleasure and success!

SUPPORTING DIFFICULT OR SAD LIFE MOMENTS

Rose quartz, the stone of unconditional love, clears and strengthens the heart energy centre, which allows for the healing of old emotional conditioning that holds you back from your full open-hearted potential. Rose quartz will also help you to navigate difficult moments of sadness or grief, release anxieties that are preventing you from moving forward and create trust in yourself and others. It encourages kindness, as when you operate from a healed heart-space you will think more clearly and be more at ease, more understanding and accepting of others and generally happier. Rose quartz is one of the most important crystals when it comes to crystal healing.

TRY THIS RITUAL: hold rose quartz over your heart and close your eyes. Visualise the energy of the crystal growing larger and larger until you are enveloped by the beautiful glowing pink light. Allow this energy to help you release any grief, sadness, anger or resentment and fill you with only peace and love.

CHAPTER 3

CHOOSING
YOUR
CRYSTALS

Have you ever heard someone say that a crystal chose them and not the other way around, and did you wonder what that might have meant?

Each of us has varying levels of sensitivity to subtle energies, such as the ones felt from crystals. Some people feel an undeniable pull towards a particular crystal when they enter a crystal store, as though that crystal must come home with them. While some people are undoubtedly able to feel the energy of crystals, the majority of people will not share that special gift.

If you don't feel the tingles, warmth or fuzzy feelings from crystals you've heard other people describe it doesn't mean there's anything wrong with you or that you're not spiritual enough, and it certainly doesn't mean crystal healing won't work for you. These ideas are sometimes spread around in spiritual communities and make people who don't share those experiences feel 'less than' and excluded. You can't feel Wi-Fi yet it still works, it still exists. Crystal healing will work for you even if you don't physically feel it happening when you hold a crystal.

If you don't really know what you're supposed to feel or experience when you find the right crystal, consider the following suggestions when you next stop by your local crystal shop:

◈ Go with a full belly: don't go crystal shopping while you're hungry. When you go into a store filled with crystals it's best to be as grounded as possible to avoid being distracted by other sensations happening within your body, and being well fed is a good first step. Being grounded helps you to be more mindful of your own body, energy and surroundings.

◈ Centre yourself on arrival, which can be simply done by taking five slow, deep, intentional breaths that bring you back into your body and clear your mind. As you take these breaths don't focus on your surroundings; focus only on you, being in your body, feeling your feet pressed against the floor and finding your centre.

◈ If you're looking for a crystal for a specific intention then take a few moments to think about that. Hold that intention in your mind as you browse through the crystals and visualise the outcome you want to happen as though it's happening in real time. When you do this you may notice that a particular crystal, colour or area of the shop feels like the right place to be.

◈ My biggest tip and probably the one that surprises people the most is to ignore all of the printed signs that tell you the meanings of the crystals when you enter the store, which can be difficult as we are conditioned to make decisions with our analytical minds. Immerse yourself in the beauty of the stones surrounding you. Get curious while you look around and browse through the crystals you wouldn't usually be interested in. See where you are guided when you allow yourself to make a decision that is guided by your intuition, emotions and curiosity rather than being prompted.

Which crystal speaks to you?

CONNECTING WITH YOUR CRYSTALS

By simply having a crystal within your energetic field or aura means you will experience the benefits of crystal healing. Crystals have energy fields just as people do, some of which span wider than others. Wearing or holding a stone is the best way to guarantee you will receive the magical benefits of your crystals; other ways you can harness the powers of crystals are:

- ◈ through crystal programming, which is explained in more detail in Chapter 8 in the clear quartz ritual

- ◈ with crystal body grids, a crystal healing treatment whereby you lie down and certain crystals are laid over and around different areas of your body

- ◈ crystal gridding, a crystal mandala that is created with focused intention and kept in your home or workspace for a specified period of time until that intention has been achieved

- ◈ meditation with a crystal specific to the energy you want to invite into your day.

Crystal grids can be used to connect with your crystals.

IF YOU CAN HAVE ONLY ONE CRYSTAL

My philosophy is that the universe is divine and perfect, therefore, if a stone is abundantly available on this earth it must be abundantly needed. The most bountiful and versatile crystal available is quartz, an incredible stone in that unlike most other crystals it can be programmed. What this means is that it magnifies the intentions you focus into it and will hold on to that focused energy until it is cleansed or a new intention is set. If you only ever buy one crystal in your life, make it quartz.

If you decide not to program your quartz it will still have incredible properties that make it worth having in your daily routine. Quartz transmutes the energy around you into higher, stabilised energy and helps with focus, clarity, decision making and memory.

Clear quartz is one of the most versatile crystals.

CHAPTER 4

MOHS HARDNESS SCALE

Mohs Hardness Scale measures the relative hardness of a mineral, 'hardness' in this case meaning the resistance of a mineral to being scratched by 10 reference minerals. Each crystal is accorded a number from 1 to 10, with 1 (talc) being the softest and 10 (diamond) the hardest. It is important to know the hardness of a particular crystal as that can help you determine the best way to care for it as well as confirm its authenticity.

If you ever have doubts about the authenticity of your crystal you can perform what's known as a scratch test. One scenario where this would help you would be if you purchased a quartz crystal and wondered whether or not it might actually be glass. You can use a quartz crystal (Moh 7) to scratch a piece of glass (for example, a glass bottle) to confirm that the glass (Moh 5–6) is softer. If the glass doesn't scratch the quartz was not harder, and therefore it is not genuine quartz.

Any stone going up to a hardness of 5 is pretty soft, so you'll need to be extra careful with those crystals as they are more vulnerable to breakages. I wouldn't recommend placing two stones of very different hardness together; for example, don't store a selenite crystal (Moh 2) in the same pouch as a heavy and hard pyrite (Moh 6–6.5) because the selenite crystal would end up broken or covered in scratches.

CRYSTAL	HARDNESS	CRYSTAL	HARDNESS
AMAZONITE	6-6.5	LARIMAR	4.5-5
AMETHYST	7	LEPIDOLITE	2.5-3
AQUAMARINE	7.5-8	MALACHITE	3.5-4
AVENTURINE	6.5-7	MOOKAITE JASPER	7
AZURITE	3.5-4	MOONSTONE	6-6.5
BLACK TOURMALINE	7-7.5	OBSIDIAN	5.5
BLOODSTONE	7	OCEAN JASPER	7
BLUE CALCITE	3	OPAL	5.5-6.5
BLUE LACE AGATE	6.5-7	PINK TOURMALINE	7-7.5
CARNELIAN	7	PREHNITE	6-6.5
CELESTITE	3-3.5	PYRITE	6-6.5
CHAROITE	5-6	RED JASPER	6.5-7
CITRINE	7	RHODOCHROSITE	3.5-4
CLEAR QUARTZ	7	RHODONITE	5.5-6
FIRE AGATE	6-7	ROSE QUARTZ	7
FLUORITE	4	RUBY FUCHSITE	9,3
GARNET	6.5-7.5	RUTILE	7

CRYSTAL	HARDNESS	CRYSTAL	HARDNESS
HEMATITE	5.5–6.5	SELENITE	2
HOWLITE	3.5	SHUNGITE	3.5–4
IOLITE	7–7.5	SMOKY QUARTZ	7
JADE	6–7	SODALITE	5.5–6
KUNZITE	6.5–7	SUNSTONE	6–6.5
KYANITE	4.5–7	TIGER'S EYE	6.5–7
LABRADORITE	6–6.5	TURQUOISE	5–6
LAPIS LAZULI	5–5.5	UNAKITE	6.5–7

Turquoise is
5–6 on Mohs
Hardness Scale.

CHAPTER 5

CLEANSING AND CARE OF YOUR CRYSTALS

Crystals need cleansing because they hold the energetic charge of anyone and anything they come into contact with. When you call on the crystal kingdom for healing, emotional support and spiritual guidance you are developing an incredibly intimate relationship. These natural tools are entrusted with your innermost secrets and desires so it's critical to give thanks to your crystal allies, showing gratitude and respect through regular cleansing, charging and care. Knowing what can damage your crystals and thus the optimum ways to care for them is also very important.

As you delve into the world of spirituality you'll learn that it's all about an equal exchange of energy: the more you give the more you will receive in return. Your crystals will increasingly become in tune with your energy and serve you better because of it. You must energetically cleanse your crystals so they are working to their maximum potential. When crystals are used as tools in healing and manifesting, a cleanse for them is like a long, hot shower after a hard day at work.

There are many methods for cleansing, but it is important that you feel connected to whatever ritual you undertake. There is no need to use all of the methods outlined in this chapter, nor should you feel restricted to always using the same method of cleansing. Change it up whenever you feel guided to.

Crystals have been used by humans for centuries but they existed long before humans ever thought to use them for healing. Who cleansed them before we did, and did they need to be cleansed? Crystals have the ability to cleanse themselves over time, just as our bodies have the natural ability to heal themselves. However, cleansing a crystal allows for the energy to be regenerated rapidly, just as healthy eating and exercise give our immune systems a boost. Furthermore, cleansing is not always about removing negative energy; sometimes it is about renewing the energy of a crystal after it has been left stagnant and unmoved for long periods of time.

There are many ways you can cleanse your crystals.

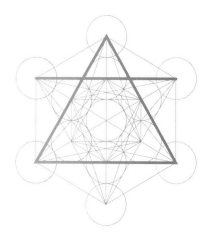

VISUALISATION CLEANSING WITH THE ELEMENT OF AIR

It is entirely possible to use the power of thought to cleanse your crystals. Find a quiet, comfortable place to sit where you will be undisturbed, hold your crystal in your hands and close your eyes. Allow the silence and serenity to envelope you and your crystal. Take slow, deep breaths and begin your visualisation cleanse when you feel that you are grounded and centred. Keeping your eyes closed, picture your crystal in front of you in your mind's eye. Visualise a divine shimmering white light coming from above and pouring over the crystal. Watch as the light washes away any negative energy trapped inside the crystal: it may look as though the crystal is slowly getting brighter and brighter, or perhaps it will look as though a dark cloud is escaping the crystal and evaporating. Perhaps you will feel it more than you see it. However it looks or feels to you will be an individual experience, but trust the process and trust also that you will feel a sense of completion when the job is done.

This ritual can take anywhere between 5 and 30 minutes depending on the crystal and how long it has been since it has been cleansed. It may take longer if you are feeling depleted or distracted. Consider your body to be a conduit for energy, transmitting and receiving information. Just as crystals need cleansing and recharging, so do you. If you aren't fully charged you have less to give, and your signal won't be as strong or as accurate. It's important to feel at peace, energised and focused when using visualisation for cleansing. If you are not in the right headspace or aren't feeling physically optimal, it may be best to try a different cleansing ritual.

SMOKE CLEANSING WITH THE ELEMENTS OF AIR, FIRE AND EARTH

The centuries-old ritual of cleansing with smoke has spanned across all corners of the earth. With traditions of smoke cleansing existing in almost every culture, it's no wonder it is one of the most commonly used crystal cleansing rituals. Think of smoke as an energetic reset button. It is a powerful magical combination of the elements of air, fire and earth, elements that when merged allow for the neutralisation and recreation of the energy in the space they inhabit.

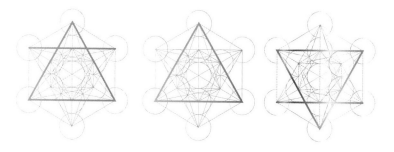

If you can accept that all crystals emanate their own unique energies that interplay and shape your own, it makes sense that all other elements of nature, including plants, can do the same thing. Plants have their own metaphysical properties, so when you blend herbs for your own smoke ritual you should consider all of these qualities and adapt the plants you use for your individual needs. Following are a couple of different ways you can use smoke to cleanse your crystals.

◈ *With a herb wand*: bind a bundle of herbs together with a natural string such as 100 per cent cotton or hemp to create a herbal wand. Your wand could include plants such as, but not limited to, lavender flowers, rosemary sprigs, rose petals and bay leaves. Light the end of the bundle with a match, candle or lighter and blow out the flame once the bundle begins to smoulder. Move through your space and allow the smoke to pass over your crystals and your home. As you do this you might choose to say a prayer or give thanks to the spirit of the plant, which will give your ritual more meaning and enhance its power.

◈ *In a dish or cauldron*: light a small charcoal disc and place it in a fire-safe dish or cauldron. Once you have chosen which herbs and resins you wish to burn, sprinkle a small amount over the coal. As the smoke rises out of the cauldron you can hold each crystal one by one, passing them through the smoke and allowing the energy to be cleansed. A standard charcoal disc will burn for approximately 30 minutes. If need be you can light another disc and add more herbs until you have completed your smoke cleansing. My favourite herbal combination for burning in a small cauldron is frankincense, rose petals and cinnamon.

Note: whether you use the smoke of incense, wood, sacred plants or home-grown herbs, be sure to harvest or source your burning ingredients sustainably and with respect. Also, never leave a flame unattended, always use a fire-safe bowl or plate and be careful not to inhale the smoke, ensuring all windows and doors are open to allow the smoke to clear out of the room.

Incense can be used for cleansing your crystals.

WATER CLEANSING WITH THE ELEMENT OF WATER

Water is a powerful cleansing tool that is freely provided by Mother Nature. It is purifying, both literally and energetically, for both humans and crystals. However, it's crucial to understand that not all crystals can tolerate exposure to water, that some crystals cannot be placed in water because they are too soft or brittle. Water may cause some crystals to fracture and break, or even dissolve. Ensure your crystals are not at risk of damage if you decide to use water for cleansing your crystals. This is by no means an exhaustive list, but in general the following stones can be water cleansed without risk of damage: amber, amethyst, blue lace agate, carnelian, citrine, moldavite, obsidian, quartz, rose quartz, smoky quartz and shungite. Be sure to look up your crystal and which cleansing method is best for it, but following are a couple of examples.

◈ *In the ocean*: salt is used as an ingredient not only in cooking but also in ritual work, and is known the world over for its protective and cleansing properties. Take your crystals to the beach with you. You may find it is useful to keep smaller crystals in a pouch together, making them easier to hold on to and less likely you will lose them in the ocean. Hold the crystals so they are fully immersed in the water, pausing for a moment to give thanks to both the crystals for their healing and to the ocean for its cleansing; this can be either in your mind or out loud. There is no set standard of time for the ritual; however, as a guide until you feel more confident in your own intuition you can begin with a timeframe of 2 minutes. If you're confident and sensitive to crystal energy, when you feel the shift in energy remove the crystals. As you take them out of the ocean be sure to follow up by rinsing them using clean fresh water before putting them away.

◈ *Running water*: hold your crystal under running tap water or in a stream or pour bottled water over them if you don't have access to any other water. It is important to keep your intention focused in your mind so, as you do this, hold a strong intention for the energy of the crystal to be cleansed and for any unwanted energies to be washed away.

Place your crystals under moonlight for cleansing.

MOONLIGHT CLEANSING

This is arguably the most frequently used method for cleansing crystals and also the easiest, as it is safe for all crystals. If you're a little forgetful when it comes to cleansing your crystals a full moon can act as a monthly reminder that it is time. Simply wait for the full moon and place your crystals outside so they are surrounded by the moon's cleansing energy. If you don't have an outdoor area that is safe for your crystals to be placed a windowsill will work just as well. It doesn't matter if your window isn't facing the moon; the moon's energy will still be present. Leave your crystals in the moonlight overnight and bring them back inside in the morning. It is done.

CARING FOR YOUR CRYSTALS

The safest place to keep your crystals is in your home. Rare mineral specimens and museum-grade collectible crystals should always be kept inside a glass cabinet to protect them. You may find they collect a lot of dust if they are left out on shelves or around the home and, depending on the mineral, the less it is unnecessarily handled the better. As for commercial-grade, harder and more robust crystals such as quartz, keeping them around the home is fine. If you find they become dusty and you want to clean them without exposing them to water, try using a large, soft paintbrush to brush the dust out from the crevices within your crystal clusters.

Exposure to water and sunlight can sometimes be damaging to crystals. It's always recommended that you carry out research before exposing your minerals to these conditions to avoid the disappointment of ruining your crystal collection.

◈ *Water exposure risk*: some minerals will dissolve or lose their lustre when exposed to water, while others will leach out toxins and can be dangerous when wet. Some minerals can even rust if exposed to water. As a starting point you can refer to the Mohs Hardness Scale guide in Chapter 4. Generally speaking, crystals with a hardness of 6 and up can usually tolerate water exposure without risk of damage. However, this is not a reliable indicator of whether or not a mineral can safely be exposed to water and does not negate the risk of toxins leaching into the water. It does, though, give you a foundation to begin determining that a crystal is unsafe in water if it is a very soft stone. One of the rare exceptions to this rule is shungite, which is completely safe to expose to water.

Stones that should never be exposed to water are azurite, blue calcite, celestite, fluorite, kunzite, kyanite, labradorite, lapis lazuli, lepidolite, malachite, pyrite, ruby fuchsite, rutile (on its own rutile shouldn't be exposed to water, but if included inside quartz it is fine), selenite and tiger's eye.

Fluorite should never be exposed to water.

◈ *Sunlight exposure risk*: the main risk of exposing crystals to sunlight is that some minerals will lose their vibrant colour over time or become sun bleached. Conversely, some minerals can become darkened by sunlight and look cooked, which is a more common issue with stones that are gemmy or have transparency although some opaque crystals can also be affected by sunlight. None of this means you can never take your crystals outdoors; exposure to sunlight for short periods of time is perfectly fine. The concern arises more so when crystals are left in sunlight for extended periods.

Stones that are at higher risk for being bleached or damaged by sunlight are amethyst, aquamarine, aventurine, blue calcite, blue lace agate, carnelian, celestite, citrine, fluorite, iolite, kunzite, larimar, lepidolite, moonstone, opal, pink tourmaline, prehnite, rhodochrosite, rose quartz, rutile, selenite and smoky quartz.

There is a risk aquamarine will be bleached by sunlight.

This is by no means an exhaustive list, but I hope these cleansing and care suggestions will help you to protect your collection and give you a foundation from which to continue learning.

CHAPTER 6

CRYSTALS IN YOUR HOME

Your home is your sanctuary, a place to retreat from the outside world and a space that is entirely your own. The way you spend time in your home and the things you place in it have a significant effect on the energy you create there. When you are choosing how to place your crystals in your home it's vital to consider how the energies of those crystals might influence the space. Many people keep all of their crystals in one place such as the bedroom, and while that might be convenient it's not always the best course of action. This usually stems from the belief that crystals have good energy, and lots of good energy in one place can't be bad, right?

As with anything in life, however, everything is best in moderation. A large group of crystals in close proximity will emanate large amounts of high vibrational frequencies in the room they are in, so if they are in your bedroom they could negatively impact your ability to have deep, restorative sleep. High-vibe crystals near your bed could cause overactive third eye and crown chakras, which could lead to excessive vivid or lucid dreaming or astral projection. While that may seem cool at first, I can assure you that after a while it is exhausting. Deep sleep is a key ingredient to a healthy life.

My philosophy is that if you have the space to do so it is best to spread your crystals out around your home according to the energy you want to cultivate in each particular room. If you don't have the space to do so or you need to keep your crystals in one place together, place them in a more neutral area of the home such as the living room.

Here are some suggestions for each room in the house:

- ◈ *Bedroom*: celestite, howlite, larimar, lepidolite, rose quartz, salt lamp.

- ◈ *Child's bedroom*: moonstone, rose quartz, salt lamp, selenite.

- ◈ *Bathroom*: amethyst, clear quartz cluster, jade.

- ◈ *Kitchen*: carnelian, clear quartz, pyrite, rose quartz.

- ◈ *Living room*: amethyst, clear quartz cluster, malachite, rose quartz.

- ◈ *Office*: citrine, fluorite, lapis lazuli, shungite, rutile, smoky quartz.

- ◈ *Entry*: black tourmaline, obsidian, selenite.

CHAPTER 7

CRYSTAL ELIXIRS

A crystal elixir is a potion that's made by placing a crystal in water so the water can be energetically charged by the crystal's unique frequency. The charged water can be used in many ways; however, the main uses are as drinking water or to bless a space. While crystal elixirs have gained in popularity over the years it's important to know that not all crystals are safe to use in elixirs, nor are all crystals that are safe to use in elixirs safe to drink.

Many crystals are made up of harmful elements such as copper, aluminium, sulphur, arsenic, lead and more. When placed in water these crystals can leach out toxins and make the water unsafe for consumption or handling. There is no need to be afraid of holding your crystals upon learning this; after all, knowledge is empowering, and now that you know this you're equipped to create crystal rituals that you can be confident are safe and effective! The majority of crystals sold in the commercial space are safe for use on a daily basis in standard crystal-healing methods such as carrying and crystal body grids and for placing around your home.

Amber is safe to use in elixirs.

It is best to use polished crystals in elixirs.

Please note that when using crystals for an elixir you should only ever use a polished form, and that it is important there are no other crystals or minerals present in that particular piece. These crystals are safe to use in a crystal elixir:

◈ amber
◈ amethyst
◈ blue lace agate
◈ carnelian

◈ citrine
◈ moldavite
◈ obsidian
◈ quartz

◈ rose quartz
◈ smoky quartz
◈ shungite.

TIP: before using your crystal elixir, remove the crystal from the water and ensure that no pieces have broken off and have been left in the water.

CHAPTER 8

CRYSTAL
RITUALS

When they first discover them many people find themselves suddenly enamoured by crystals. It's not uncommon for a crystal enthusiast to build a huge collection, fall in love with all of the metaphysical properties and then feel disheartened by the little time they have to use their crystals. We all have busy schedules and it's hard to make time to energetically work with all of our crystals, so the best way to get the most out of our crystals is to incorporate them into daily rituals.

WHAT IS A RITUAL?

The word 'ritual' usually invokes imagery of naked women dancing around a flame under the moonlight or bones scattered across a velvet tablecloth lit by candles, but this is not always the case. Often when you think of what a ritual is the assumption is that it's always a formal ceremony wrought with occult undertones and sacrifices. While these may represent some types of rituals, in the modern world we understand that our magic can culminate in the more mundane rituals of our everyday lives. After all, the routines we follow and repeat every day ultimately make up the ritual of our lives.

Every day when you wake up and check your phone, do morning yoga, drink a coffee or catch the bus you are partaking in the rituals of your daily life. Everything you do is ritual; it is a part of the human experience. Your life is a series of rituals, and every choice you make is an ingredient and every word you speak a spell. The outcome depends on the rituals you choose to engage in. Once you realise this you see the world and your experience of it through a different lens.

When you are seeking change in your life you need to be willing to alter your daily rituals. You have to acknowledge and establish in your mind that the rituals you are doing are not yielding the results you desire then, once you do this, you'll be left with the question of which rituals will give you the results you want.

Let's take one example of a common daily ritual that could be adjusted to improve your life: looking at your phone every morning.

If you're experiencing stress, anxiety and/or poor self-esteem the ritual of looking at social media as soon as you wake up every morning is not going to benefit you. You know this deep down yet you still do it. How committed are you to changing your rituals to improve your life? The first thoughts to enter your consciousness every morning are vital to your state of mind for the rest of the day, and every thought that comes afterwards alters the chemicals in your body, the internal stories you tell yourself and ultimately the decisions that you make.

It's dangerous for a healthy state of mind to wake up and think 'I'm fat and ugly' and then look at social media and be bombarded by images of thin people whom you compare yourself to. If you do this every morning you're putting an immense amount of stress on yourself and telling yourself over and over again that you're not enough, that there is something wrong with you and that other people are better than you because of their size or appearance. This form of thinking is not only detrimental to your mental health but also to your physical and energetic health.

Change your daily ritual to change your life! Take control of your mind, body and spirit by interrupting the repetitive thoughts that enter your mind and persuade you to make unhealthy choices. Instead, when you wake up in the morning meditate with a calming crystal such as amethyst and write down some positive words in your journal to set the tone for the day. To give you a head start use these phrases, which you can say out loud or in your head:

I am beautiful.
I am grateful for my body.
I am healthy.
I am enough.
I welcome positive experiences.
Today is going to be a beautiful day.
I allow myself to be happy.
I love myself and I am deserving of love.
I am in control of my life.
I am brave enough to be myself.
The world is full of incredible opportunities for me.

When you replace your morning ritual with positive journaling you are rewriting the story of your life and manifesting the positive and healthy feelings and experiences you deserve. Show the universe you are ready for a change by inviting it in with an open door in the form of old habits being erased.

Here are a few suggestions to inspire you to incorporate crystals in daily rituals:

- ◈ Place your trusty selenite crystal under your bed so you enjoy a restful sleep and wake up feeling refreshed.

- ◈ Give voice to morning affirmations with your intuitively chosen daily crystal.

- ◈ Have a crystal gua sha face massage after cleansing to leave your skin glowing.

- ◈ Spritz a crystal-infused energy clearing spray around to start your day right.

- ◈ Wear gemstone jewellery to carry the energy of your favourite stones throughout the day.

- ◈ Place a crystal at your desk to keep you grounded and focused at work.

- ◈ To wind down after a big day and stay centred, try some crystal meditation.

MANIFESTING RITUALS

When you manifest you are utilising your energy to its fullest potential to create a reality for yourself where your goals, plans and desires are all attracted into your life. The energy you build around yourself is like a magnet, and you can use that magnetism to intentionally create your reality, write your own story and manifest your dreams. Crystals are incredible tools that help to manipulate the energy of a space by constantly emanating a specific frequency. When you incorporate crystals into your manifesting rituals you amplify and accelerate the potency of your ritual and ultimately your potential outcome. The stones most commonly used in manifesting rituals, which attract abundance and prosperity, amplify intentions and accelerate manifesting power among many other things, include:

- *Citrine*, for attracting abundance and happiness.

- *Clear quartz*, for amplifying your intentions and keeping your mind focused.

- *Hematite*, for bringing your ideas into the physical world.

- *Pyrite*, for attracting wealth.

- *Rutile*, for amplifying and accelerating manifesting energy.

You are not limited to these stones when you manifest with crystals; trust your intuition and allow it to guide you to the crystals

Use citrine to attract abundance and happiness.

that complement the energy you are cultivating in your life. When you begin your journey of manifesting with crystals you will quickly learn that you yield the best results when you are more conscious of the thoughts you allow into your mind. Energy attracts energy, and frequency will find a matching frequency.

Imagine the world is made up of billions of tiny invisible webs, pathways for energy to travel and meet up. When you manifest it is like you are strumming on one of those strings and sending out an energetic beacon, inviting that same energy back to you. It is a call and response, which is why your thoughts are so crucial to achieving the best possible results and also the reason that the crystals listed are not the only useful crystals for manifesting.

Crystal journaling ritual for manifesting with gratitude

Make your intentional thoughts a ritual practice. For the most beneficial outcome you must be willing to do this ritual as a daily practice rather than as a one-time event. By committing to this ritual you have the potential to change your entire life.

You will need a pen, journal and rutile crystal. When you wake up every morning, spend 10 minutes contemplating the miracle of life while you hold on to your rutile crystal. Think about all of the things you are grateful for and take a moment to give thanks, either out loud or in your mind, to some higher power for showering you with such blessings. This higher power can be whatever you choose; it does not need to be a religious figure. Perhaps your gratitude will be extended to the universe, the earth, spirit or your ancestors.

While you are focusing on all you are thankful for, write these things down. When you put it out to the universe that the life you have is received with gratitude and love you communicate energetically to say 'Thank you, I accept these gifts.' Accepting the gifts is an invitation to receive more, which will be further amplified by your rutile crystal. Gratitude is a high vibrational frequency to hold and one that is magnetic. Your ability to draw in the things you want in life will be magnified when you give thanks for what you have. Keep your rutile crystal with your journal so it can emanate its own energy as well as the manifesting and abundant energy of the words in your journal.

If you are not sure where your gratitude should begin, try these prompts to get you started:

> *I am grateful for the gift of life.*
> *I am grateful for the privilege of ageing.*
> *I am grateful for clean water and food.*
> *I am grateful for the sound of rain.*
> *I am grateful for my hearing, sight and voice.*

Money ritual

Simply keep a small citrine crystal in your wallet or purse to attract wealth and prosperity.

Planting seeds ritual

Take four quartz crystals and some seeds to sow in your garden. With each seed plant a quartz crystal and set an intention for what you wish to manifest in your life, making it one specific intention for each crystal and seed pair. You can label your intention along with the label of your plant so you remember what each seed symbolises. As your plants grow your manifested intentions will come to life. Tend to them in the garden, watering them and watching them flourish.

Resume ritual

Are you applying for a new job or promotion? Whether you have applied with a hard copy or digital application or filled out a form, print a copy of the application so you can work your manifesting magic. Place your application on your altar with a pyrite crystal on top of it to amplify the determined and ambitious energy you are transmitting to your new job.

Close to your heart ritual

In the morning as you get dressed and prepare for the day tuck a unakite and rose quartz crystal into your bra to amplify the loving energies surrounding your heart chakra. As you do this, hold the intention that you will attract a new

Carry rose quartz close to your heart.

love into your life. Manifest love by inviting this energy into your life and opening your heart to a new relationship. If you do not wear a bra or find this uncomfortable you can opt to wear a crystal necklace that hangs low over your chest.

Set fire to your fears ritual

Fears and self-limiting beliefs get in the way of you achieving your goals and manifesting your dream future. Think about what big goal you are hoping to manifest and write down all of the fears you have surrounding that goal, such as:

> *What is the worst-case scenario?*
> *Why won't it happen for me?*
> *What's getting in my way?*
> *How would my life change if I achieved it, and what about that scares me?*

When you're finished, fold the paper and place a black tourmaline crystal on it to absorb and transmute all the low-vibrational energy surrounding your goals. When you're ready to release these fears, burn the paper in a fire-safe environment and release all of the energetic blockage that is preventing you from manifesting your goals into life!

PROTECTION RITUALS

Everyone wants to feel safe and protected, so there could be many reasons why you turned to this section of the book. For some people protection rituals are a preventative daily practice, while for others they are rituals performed in response to an event. Protection rituals can help guard you against unwanted energy that has been sent your way, can rid you of the energetic remnants left on you after a difficult day or can give you courage and a sense of preparedness for stepping into challenging situations. Whatever the reason for performing a crystal ritual for protection, it's always beneficial to begin with the understanding that everything is energy, and energy can be transmuted. With this in mind you can step into your ritual without fear, knowing that you have the power to transform any low-vibrational, discordant energies into higher-vibrational, usable energy. Crystals can be used to create energetic boundaries so that unusable or undesirable energy does not interfere with your daily life.

Black tourmaline absorbs negative energy.

The stones most commonly used in protection rituals purify your energy, absorb negative energy and deflect ill wishes, among many other things. They include:

◈ *Black tourmaline*, for absorbing negative energy and transmuting it.

◈ *Black obsidian*, for deflecting negative energy.

◈ *Labradorite*, for guarding your energy from being drained.

◈ *Selenite*, for its purifying and cleansing properties and bringing divine light energy into a space.

You are not limited to these stones when you use crystals in protection rituals. Trust your intuition and allow it to guide you to the crystals that will best suit the type of protection you require at a particular moment.

Protecting your home crystal grid ritual

Begin this ritual by cleaning your home, as energy can become trapped in untidy places. The best results will be achieved by starting with a clean space. Also, cleanse your crystals by using one of the cleansing rituals outlined in Chapter 5.

Place one black obsidian crystal by the front entrance of your home to ensure that negative energy stops at the front door. Place one black tourmaline crystal and one selenite crystal together in each of the four furthest corners of your home to ensure there is a linked barrier around the perimeter. Place them out of reach where they won't be moved by pets, children or curious visitors. If you want to enhance this ritual you could use more than four sets of tourmaline and selenite, placing them in all of the rooms in your home. However, four sets are a great starting point and are perfectly sufficient.

Placing black tourmaline and selenite in your home ensures that low-vibe energy will be transmuted into positivity. Black tourmaline absorbs negative energy while selenite has incredible purifying qualities, and by pairing them you're ensuring the black tourmaline is kept cleansed and the selenite is helping to introduce high-vibrational energy into your home.

Selenite.

Psychic protection ritual

Do you ever feel like someone else is in your energy field, that maybe they know things they shouldn't? You can feel their presence when they're not around or your intuition has warned you that your energy is being influenced by another person's energy. Sometimes people can unintentionally enter your energy field simply by thinking of you often and holding on to jealousy towards you or gossiping about you, and sometimes they can intentionally enter your energy field to interfere with your success or wish you misfortune.

To guard against this, sit on the floor with your legs crossed and use black tourmaline, blue kyanite, labradorite, obsidian and selenite to form a circle around you. Meditate inside your crystal circle, where you are surrounded by the protective and balancing energies emanating from your crystal allies. Take deep breaths as you meditate, holding on to the intention of clearing your energy field of other people or anything that is draining you.

Breathe in the restorative energies of the labradorite and kyanite, directing their healing properties to your third eye chakra. Breathe out the blockages or attachments in you that are linking you to anyone else and causing disharmony in your body, directing this energy into the selenite, black tourmaline and obsidian. Allow them to absorb, transmute and purify the energy.

All the while the crystals will be protecting you from any further influence entering into your aura.

Protective amulet ritual

Wearing a special piece of jewellery made with crystals for protection not only helps to guard your energy but can also make you feel indestructible. This shift in perspective adds to the potency of your ritual – never underestimate the power that can be accumulated by your mental and emotional states.

Because jewellery is worn against your body for long periods of time the connection between you and your protection amulet is more potent than that of a new crystal that simply sits on a desk or is meditated with only occasionally. An amulet becomes an extension of you, and as time goes by the bond between you and your amulet will grow and you will feel a difference when you wear it. Embark on a ritual of putting on your amulet every morning after you have dressed for the day and, as you do so, visualise the amulet creating a protective force field around you. Think of the amulet as energetic armour that you don before stepping into the arena of life. Choose an amulet that incorporates one or more of the following crystals for the best results: amethyst, black tourmaline, clear quartz, obsidian or selenite.

Obsidian works well for an amulet.

ENERGETIC HEALTH RITUALS

Maintaining energetic health will ensure you live a happy and robust life. Your energetic, emotional, spiritual and physical levels all come together to form the temple that is your body, and when there is discordance on any of those levels it will have a domino effect on the others. You can work with crystals to ensure your energetic health is always at its optimum using the below rituals as a guide for creating your own routine for energetic health.

Healthy office environment ritual

If you work in an office, at a computer all day or surrounded by technology it's possible your energetic health is being influenced by the amount of electromagnetic radiation you are exposed to. In the modern world it's near impossible to go through a day without exposure to electronic magnetic fields (EMFs), Wi-Fi, Bluetooth and the like, and I imagine you would rather not have the exposure. These things make your life more convenient and allow you to connect to the rest of the world at the click of a button, but that doesn't mean you can't implement small changes in your space to ensure your energy is protected from the new technologically enhanced reality.

The best crystals to use to support your energetic health in EMF environments include black tourmaline, fluorite, shungite, smoky quartz and sodalite. Keep yourself grounded and allow these crystals to support your energy by placing them around your office or workspace.

Take time at least once a week to cleanse your crystals so they can continue to work at their maximum capacity and to thank them for supporting your energetic health. See Chapter 5 for more information on cleansing your crystals.

Exhale the day ritual

You may choose to do this ritual daily, weekly or only on certain days when you feel drawn to do so. Whatever frequency you decide, this ritual is a great way to decompress and release any stressful blockages that are causing disharmony in your energy body, and the best part is its simplicity.

Have one purifying crystal dedicated to this ritual such as black tourmaline, obsidian, selenite or shungite. Sit in a quiet place with your purifying crystal and take deep breaths. Hold the crystal up to your mouth as you exhale, directing released energies into it. When you are done, cleanse your crystal and thank it for helping you to bring your energy back into harmony.

Black tourmaline and shungite are purifying crystals.

PSYCHIC DEVELOPMENT RITUALS

Let's just start with this, shall we: *you are psychic*. There is no doubt in my mind that every soul on this green earth has a psychic gift. It is a muscle that must be exercised, and with enough care and attention that muscle will grow in strength. For the sake of sticking with the metaphorical theme, think of crystals as being the dumb-bells of your psychic exercise routine: sure, you can enhance your intuition without them but why not have a little help?

The crystals most commonly used in psychic development rituals open your psychic channels, enhance your communication with the divine and strengthen your intuition, among many other things. They include:

- ◈ amethyst

- ◈ azurite

- ◈ iolite

- ◈ lapis lazuli

- ◈ sodalite.

Azurite.

You are not limited to these stones when you use crystals for enhancing your psychic abilities. Trust your instincts and allow your intuition to guide you to the crystals that will best suit the psychic support you need.

Card a day ritual

Using divination cards is an excellent way to enhance your psychic development, and it doesn't matter whether you're more inclined towards oracle, reading or tarot cards. Using any of these will allow you to exercise your psychic muscles and open up your senses to receiving information from beyond. When you work with divination cards you become a conduit for messages from the divine.

Create a daily ritual of selecting one card each morning, then spend the day reflecting on the card you selected and how it might be guiding you or sending you a message to improve your life. Your card readings will be enhanced if you hold on to an amethyst, azurite, iolite, labradorite, lapis lazuli or sodalite crystal.

Enhance your card-reading skills by incorporating crystals.

Enhance your psychic dreams ritual

Place an amethyst crystal in your pillowcase to encourage the opening of your psychic channels while you are sleeping. Amethyst is a catalyst for consciousness expansion and will encourage your psychic senses to open up and receive messages through your dreams.

Open your psychic channels with amethyst.

Crystal gazing

The notion of crystal gazing usually engenders images of someone gazing into a crystal ball. A quartz crystal ball is a wonderful crystal to use for gazing, but crystal gazing can be done on any crystal that has a reflective surface such as a clear quartz crystal ball, a polished slice of obsidian or a seer stone.

Hold the crystal in front of you or place it on a table in front of you at eye level. Gaze into the crystal and allow your mind to enter a psychic state. Pay attention to the images that enter your mind. As you develop this skill it will be helpful for you to keep a notepad nearby so that afterwards you can mark down what you remember, which is an excellent way to exercise your psychic abilities.

AMAZONITE:
MORNING HARMONY RITUAL

The amazonite morning harmony ritual is a perfect way to start your day as it will guide you into a centred and harmonious energetic space. This ritual, which is best performed first thing in the morning, requires you to do some preparation the evening beforehand. You will need:

◈   1 amazonite crystal

◈   1 tablespoon of dried jasmine flowers

◈   a small charcoal disc

◈   a small cauldron or fire-proof bowl matches or a lighter.

Before you go to sleep, place the amazonite crystal on the jasmine flowers so its calming vibrations can entwine with the meditative qualities of jasmine. When you wake in the morning open the window, place the charcoal disc in the cauldron, light it and sprinkle it with the jasmine flowers. Hold on to your amazonite and begin your day with a 20-minute morning meditation or until the incense has burned through. If you find your mind wandering while you meditate, acknowledge the intruding thought and bring your focus back to the intention of having a glorious, harmonious day. And you will!

AMETHYST:
PUT IT TO REST RITUAL

For this ceremonial burial for your worries you will need:

- an amethyst tumbled stone

- pen and paper

- a small biodegradable box

- a spade.

   Sit with the amethyst crystal in one hand and the pen in the other and take a moment to reflect on the worries that are occupying your mind and distracting you from inner peace. As each worry passes your mind write it down on the paper and say 'I release you.' Take your time and be specific. With each release you will feel lighter. Once you have written down all of your current worries, fold the paper and place it inside the biodegradable box. Thank the crystal for its support and place it on the paper. Seal the box shut, dig a hole with the spade in a place that won't be disturbed and bury the box, noting that it shouldn't be on your property. Once you have covered the box with the earth's soil, take a moment to say goodbye then leave your worries behind for good.

   It is done.

AQUAMARINE:
OCEAN RENEWAL RITUAL

There is nothing quite like swimming in the ocean, being engulfed in the immeasurable salt water and floating under the sun as the light is reflected and refracted all around you. Salt water is incredibly healing. When you feel it is time to renew your life force, cleanse your emotions and purify any stagnant energy held in your body, head to the ocean. Take your aquamarine with you so it may be cleansed alongside you, and immerse it and your whole body in the salt water to receive the healing power of the sea. Afterwards, rinse your aquamarine in fresh water so the salt does not damage it. If you can't get to the ocean or are unable to swim you could put sea salt in your bath water for a similar effect.

It's best to take only a small polished aquamarine such as a tumbled stone into the ocean with you as a raw mineral specimen could be damaged by water. It's also advisable to place your aquamarine in a drawstring bag or something similar so you can hold on to it more easily and don't lose it.

Use aquamarine to cleanse your emotions.

BLACK TOURMALINE:
RETURN TO SENDER RITUAL

Undertake this ritual if you sense your energy field is being influenced by another person against your will. You will need:

◈   1 black candle

◈   5 black tourmaline crystals

◈   a pen

◈   1 bay leaf or a small piece of paper

◈   a cauldron or fire-safe bowl.

Make a circle around the candle with the black tourmaline crystals. Before you light the candle, take a moment to think about the events happening around you: what events led you to do this ritual? Once you have that in mind light the candle. Write the words 'I return these unwanted energies to sender' on the bay leaf or paper, close your eyes and visualise unwanted energy being lifted from you. Open your eyes and feel the energy start to shift. Light the leaf with the candle and place it in the bowl to safely burn the whole way through.

It is done.

BLUE CALCITE:
UNLOCKING YOUR INSPIRATION RITUAL

Whether you're having trouble with writer's block, struggling to communicate your thoughts or feel uninspired, this ritual can help to unblock any energy that's getting in your way. You will need:

- ◈ 1 blue calcite crystal

- ◈ calming music

- ◈ a notebook or paper and pen.

Meditate with the crystal while you listen to some peaceful or inspiring music. Close your eyes and hold the crystal in your hands. Visualise the soft blue colour expanding out of the crystal and enveloping you and hold this visualisation for at least 5 minutes while you take deep breaths. Notice how it makes you feel: do you feel cool, warm, tingling, calm? When you're ready to move on, hold the crystal over your brow and allow its energy to stimulate your third eye chakra. Next bring the crystal to your throat, as the connection between these two areas of your body will be strengthened by the blue calcite.

Place the crystal in the centre of the paper and draw lines on it as though they are radiating out from the crystal. Think of it as a brainstorm and write down any words that come to you. If you use this ritual to enhance your awareness of your emotions you could write down any feelings you are experiencing, and if you are trying to overcome a creative block you could write down any inspiration that has come to you. Do this exercise any time you feel stuck verbalising your thoughts to kick-start the expression of your unique internal experience.

CELESTITE:
PEACEFUL HOME BLESSING RITUAL

Use this ritual to shower your home with loving intentions. You will need:

◈   a bowl

◈   1 celestite crystal

◈   a cup

◈   a handful of dried lavender.

Half fill the bowl with clean water. As you fill the bowl also fill your mind with peaceful and calm thoughts, envisioning your home as a sanctuary, a safe space. Place the crystal in the cup and then place the cup in the bowl of water, being careful to not get water in the cup as it could damage the crystal. Even though the crystal is not directly touching the water, the water will still be energetically altered. Sprinkle the lavender over the water and allow the lavender and crystal energy to steep into the water for at least 10 minutes.

During this time you may choose to meditate beside the bowl, holding the intention of a love-filled, serene home. When you are ready, take the cup out of the bowl and carry the bowl through all areas of your home. As you move through your home dip your hand into the water and sprinkle it all around. Say in your mind or out loud 'In my home I am safe. In my home I am at peace.' Pour any remaining water outside the doors to your home.

Bring peace into your home with celestite.

CLEAR QUARTZ:
PROGRAMMING YOUR CRYSTAL RITUAL

Programming your quartz is a simple ritual that should still be done with reverence for the best results. Take a few deep breaths to quiet your mind then cleanse your quartz in whatever way you feel intuitively guided to do. Hold your quartz crystal, or place it in front of you and hold your hands over it with your palms facing down. Hold on to one focused intention and visualise the energy moving through you and transferring into the crystal. Do this for a few minutes until you feel the ritual is complete.

Some examples of intentions you could set are the motivation to exercise regularly or for mental clarity, emotional healing and peaceful dreams or to manifest a new job. Your options are limitless.

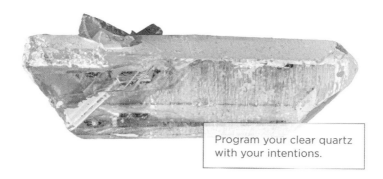

Program your clear quartz with your intentions.

GARNET:

MINDFULNESS VISUALISATION RITUAL

Find a quiet place to collect your thoughts and centre your energy, hold your garnet crystal and close your eyes. Take a deep breath in, and as you do so visualise the beautiful energy of your garnet flowing out of the crystal and into your nose, down into your lungs, through your arms and legs and finally through the soles of your feet and into the earth. As you breathe out think about what the heaviness, stress or less-appealing energies you're feeling in your body right now might look like. Visualise them leaving your body with every exhale and dissipating into the air. Do this breathing exercise for five long, deep breaths. Now that you have grounded yourself with your garnet and your breathing, take notice of the feelings in your body. Do you feel your feet firmly pressed against the floor? Can you identify the sounds

around you? What can you smell? Open your eyes and look around quietly, observing the textures, colours and shapes that surround you.

This exercise doesn't necessarily have a set destination or moment to mark its completion; do it for as long as you need to in order to find a sense of groundedness and to feel that you have settled into the present moment. The purpose of the exercise is for you to exist in the present moment, practise mindfulness and find a quiet moment for yourself to simply exist without expectation or pressure from any outside source. Just be.

LABRADORITE:
CORD-CUTTING RITUAL

Cord cutting is an excellent practice for those who feel they take on other people's energy and emotions or have a hard time shaking off the energy of the day when they get home.

We all have invisible energetic 'cords' that link us to people in our lives or experiences we have been through and act as a pathway for energetic exchange. It's very common to have energetic cords with the people close to you, as well as people you think about frequently – both those you are fond of and those you aren't. Because of this it's a good idea to regularly reset your energy by cutting or removing cords.

If you're new to the concept of energetic cord cutting you might worry that it's a negative practice to break an energetic bond between you and the people you love, but that's not really the case. By cutting your cords you're ensuring that your energy is cleansed and you are not being energetically influenced by other people or remnant energies left over from difficult life experiences.

Find a quiet place and close your eyes as you hold your labradorite crystal. Set a strong intention to identify and then remove any unwanted energetic attachments you have within your energetic body. Visualise what a cord might look like to you: does it look like a rubber electrical cord or a string of light? Maybe yours look like leafy vines, but whatever you see is perfectly fine. Move your labradorite crystal over the areas you sense you are tied to by a cord while envisioning the crystal is a sword that is cutting the cord from your energy field so you are no longer influenced by it. Do this until you have cut all the cords you have intuitively identified and then cleanse both yourself and your labradorite.

Remove unwanted attachments with labradorite.

LEPIDOLITE:
NIGHTMARES BE GONE RITUAL

If unwanted energies are seeping into your dream world consider this ritual to cleanse your mind and space. You will need:

◈ a small amount of dried lavender

◈ 1 polished lepidolite crystal

◈ a small red drawstring pouch.

Place the lavender and lepidolite crystal in the pouch. As you pull the drawstring to close the pouch hold the intention that you are guarded and protected from any malevolent energies. Visualise your worries and fears dissipating from your aura. Place the pouch under your pillow or beside your bed and keep it there until your nightmares stop. When they do stop, cleanse your crystal and discard the dried lavender.

MOONSTONE:
NEW BEGINNINGS UNDER A FULL MOON RITUAL

Perform this ritual when you feel ready to invite change into your life, during either a new or full moon phase. Take advantage of the powerful renewing energy during these significant moon phases by bathing yourself in the energy both literally and metaphorically. You will need:

◈   bath salts

◈   a candle

◈   1 moonstone crystal

◈   a small dish.

Draw yourself a relaxing bath during a full moon or new moon phase and add the bath salts to the water. Place the candle and moonstone crystal together in the dish and put the dish in a spot where you will be able to see it while you are in the bath.

Before you get into the bath, light the candle and set your intention for moving into the new phase in your life. While you're bathing, focus on that intention and visualise the outcome you wish to occur as though it is already happening. After bathing blow out the candle and carry the moonstone crystal with you for the rest of the week.

SHUNGITE:
CHARGED WATER RITUAL

Shungite is an ancient mineral that is only found in Russia, with the largest deposit being along Lake Onega. Its composition can be made of up to 98 per cent carbon, which makes it an amazing water purifier. Beyond its physically purifying properties, if you create an elixir with shungite you  also energetically charge your water with the metaphysical properties of this wonderful crystal. Shungite water is safe to drink and can also be added to your bath water or used to spray around a room to bless the space with its magical properties.

To create shungite charged water I recommend using a 2.5 centimetre piece of elite shungite, in a water jug or large water bottle–sized container. Wash your shungite under clean running water and leave it in a clean dish under direct sunlight to dry. Once cleaned and dried, place the shungite in a water bottle or canister filled with clean water and rest for 48 hours. During this time your shungite crystal will absorb any toxins in the water as well as emanate its unique vibrational frequencies into the water. Now you can enjoy naturally purified water that has been charged with the beautiful feminine energy of shungite.

CHAPTER 9

CRYSTALS
A-Z

In this chapter you will meet
your crystal allies and learn of the
lessons they wish to impart on you.
Every crystal has its own personality,
which you will soon discover as you
become more familiar with them.
Over time your connection with your
crystals will grow and you will be able
to work with them more effectively.

AMAZONITE

ELEMENT	AFFIRMATION
water ▽	*I trust myself to make the right choices for me.*

CHAKRAS	LOCATIONS
throat, heart	Brazil, Madagascar, United States

MOHS HARDNESS	PAIRS WELL WITH
6–6.5	rose quartz, ruby fuchsite, smoky quartz

I am the crystal of profound heart, mind and soul expression, converging the energies of nurturing self-care and sensible practicality. When you find yourself endlessly searching for answers, come to me. Announcing your heart's innermost truths is sometimes more difficult than it should be, but I will support you as you search for the words buried deep within, removing the clogged confusion one thought at a time. When the feelings are undeniable and you aren't even sure what it is you have to say, my hope is to help you find the right words.

Every now and then understanding what is keeping you from making the right choices for yourself is complicated. Are you afraid you'll fail? Maybe you're afraid you'll succeed. As the saying goes: 'The truth shall set you free.' With my guidance you'll be set in motion on the path that leads to you living your authentic truth.

AMETHYST

ELEMENT
air

AFFIRMATION
I am aligned in spirit, body and mind.

CHAKRAS
third eye, crown

LOCATIONS
Bolivia, Brazil, Madagascar, Uruguay

MOHS HARDNESS
6–6.5

PAIRS WELL WITH
aventurine, azurite, charoite

I am the crystal companion for those seeking higher consciousness, for mystics who yearn to reach out with their psychic senses, expand their awareness and branch out like an invisible antenna. If you have been drawn to me you will know this feeling well. When you hold me you'll feel my energy resonating all around you. I am auric armour, shielding you from low vibrational frequencies that cause discordant confusion. Relinquish the fears and patterns that block you from your evolution.

You are awakening, and I'm here to offer my support. Although you may feel that you are wandering a labyrinth as you search for your connection to the divine, know that I am here to navigate you. Do you feel it: the deep knowing that you are a part of something so huge, so powerful, so complete? It's magical, and so are you.

AQUAMARINE

ELEMENT
water ▽

AFFIRMATION
I allow myself to explore and heal my deepest feelings.

CHAKRA
throat

LOCATIONS
Afghanistan, Brazil, Namibia, Pakistan, South Africa

MOHS HARDNESS
7.5–8

PAIRS WELL WITH
blue calcite, blue lace agate, larimar

I am the crystal inhabited by the spirit of the sea. You and I are more alike than you may know. My hope is that in time I will help you find your voice and stand in your power with grace. You are an ocean, an expansive and endless swelling of life, depth, creation and destruction. You have so much responsibility, so much to think about all the time: let the noise dissolve and evaporate. I will bring you mental clarity. You are an ocean, sometimes perfectly still, other times roaring, crashing, drowning. I will help you tame your temper; the calm will come after the storm.

When you feel like you are sinking I will remind you to let go. Release your fears and move gently, floating to the surface. Take a deep breath: everything will be okay. You are an ocean, the heavens on your horizon and the land at your feet. I enhance your inner wisdom and connection to the universe, both physically and beyond the veil. Meditate with me to explore your uncharted waters, as there is still so much to discover about yourself.

AVENTURINE

ELEMENTS
earth,
water

AFFIRMATION
I am deserving of happiness.

CHAKRA
heart

LOCATIONS
Brazil, India

MOHS HARDNESS
6.5–7

PAIRS WELL WITH
fluorite, kunzite, sunstone

I am the crystal of optimism and abundance. I am the crystal that embodies the feeling that anything is possible in the early mornings of spring. I am the light shining through the clouds after the rain. I want you to open your heart and know that you are an eternal and integral part of this world. When you take care of yourself you are taking care of everyone and everything that you love. Be kind to yourself. Put your health first, always. You can create a life that is beautiful, a life full of bliss.

Look for joy in the simple things in life such as the smell of fresh bread, flowers bursting through the pavement or the sun glistening on the face of someone you love. Optimism is a muscle that I will help you to exercise. You are deserving of happiness. If you ever feel you are facing an impossible task, come to me. Hold me close and remember: only you can decide what your next step is.

AZURITE

ELEMENT	AFFIRMATION
air △	*I am divinely connected to the universe.*

CHAKRAS	LOCATIONS
crown, third eye	Australia, Morocco, Namibia, United States

MOHS HARDNESS	PAIRS WELL WITH
3.5–4	iolite, lapis lazuli, sodalite

I am the crystal of the wind, connecting your intellectual mind and your intuitive perception. I will help you to trust the hunches you feel when you know something but you can't explain how you know it. I am a magnifying glass for your psychic gifts, teaching you to see beyond the facade of deception and separate truth from dishonesty. I encourage you to lean into your gifts, which connect you to the divine source.

Like an invisible web of electricity, your thoughts do not echo into the unknown but, rather, expand and intertwine with all the thoughts of all those who inhabit this earth. This enormous collective consciousness links you together with all living creatures, and with practice you can access information beyond this timeline. You can obtain truths that are beyond what you have ever been taught is possible.

BLACK TOURMALINE

ELEMENT		AFFIRMATION	
earth ▽		*I am safe.*	

CHAKRA		LOCATIONS	
root		Brazil, China, Madagascar, Namibia, Zambia	

MOHS HARDNESS	PAIRS WELL WITH
7–7.5	obsidian, selenite, smoky quartz

I am fiercely protective of you. I'll take on any ill will sent your way. Cleanse me regularly so I can work harder for you. Bad intentions and low vibrations cannot stand to be around me. I am an absorber, a transmuter. I feed on these energies, so you don't have to endure them. I will penetrate deep into your auric field and, like a vacuum, eliminate any energetic debris.

Wear me as an amulet so I may protect you. Place me at your front door so I may guard your home. Hold on to me when you feel uncertain and I will ground you. Carry me when you are afraid and I will remind you that you are strong and in control of your own energy.

BLOODSTONE

ELEMENT
earth

AFFIRMATION
I have the courage to move through all of life's challenges.

CHAKRA
root

LOCATIONS
Australia, Brazil, China, India, Madagascar

MOHS HARDNESS
6–6.5

PAIRS WELL WITH
hematite, jade, rhodonite

I am the crystal of courage and perseverance. I instil power in you when you are facing impossible circumstances and give you the energy to endure and overcome any situation that life throws your way. When the world seems too difficult to endure and you feel your motivation dwindling, I encourage you to appreciate the beauty and fleeting nature of our existence. I remind you not to take this life for granted, but rather to practise mindfulness and rekindle your enthusiasm for the beauty in the benign.

My hope for you is that you will find pride in your ability to overcome these struggles and peace in knowing that you have the strength and vitality to do so. Don't be stopped in your tracks when the going gets tough; take action and know that you can achieve anything you put your mind to.

BLUE CALCITE

ELEMENT	AFFIRMATION
water ▽	*I express my feelings, wants and needs with ease.*

CHACKRAS		LOCATIONS
throat, third eye		Madagascar, Mexico, South Africa

MOHS HARDNESS	PAIRS WELL WITH
3	aquamarine, celestite, kyanite

My calming energy will expand to completely surround you. Surrender to my soothing blue aura so you may find inner peace. Come to me when your ideas become jumbled and lose their way on their journey to your lips. Allow me to aid you when you're blocked from conveying the thoughts that are swirling in your mind's eye. I bind the bridge between your visions and voice.

It is my goal to gently remind you that you are holding the reins of your ideas and inspiration, those same ideas that have felt so distant will now rush down into your body and pour out of you like a fountain. You need to feel heard and understood, and accessing those feelings is the first step to achieving this connection.

BLUE LACE AGATE

ELEMENT	AFFIRMATION
water ▽	*My words hold power, so I choose them wisely.*

CHAKRA	LOCATIONS
throat	Malawi, Namibia, South Africa

MOHS HARDNESS	PAIRS WELL WITH
6.5–7	amazonite, celestite, charoite

I am the crystal confidant for dreamers who whisper their worship up into the heavens. I offer my gifts to those who speak with or wish to speak with angels and spirits who are living among us, unseen but not unheard. If you feel your prayers need amplification, turn to me. I will remind you that your words are powerful spells and every utterance is creating your world around you.

I balance and energise your throat chakra so that you may communicate thoughtfully, with intention and attention. Although you may be moved by your emotions from time to time, I want you to remember the importance of speaking gently and from the heart. I will help you to calm your thoughts when they take a negative turn and shift your perspective into one of optimism, peace and positivity.

CARNELIAN

ELEMENT	AFFIRMATION
fire	*I am the architect of my reality.*

CHAKRAS	LOCATIONS
sacral, root	Brazil, Madagascar

MOHS HARDNESS	PAIRS WELL WITH
7	fire agate, opal, tiger's eye

You have a fire burning inside of you, and although it may dim from time to time know that it never goes out. Not entirely. Not ever. I am an eternal fuel, fanning your embers until you blaze with all your power. I see incredible strength in you. More than you can imagine. Burn fearlessly: the veils of distortion and uncertainty will not survive your blinding light. Nothing can hide in the shadows.

You are a beacon, signalling action, courage and passion. My hope for you is that what no longer serves you will be devoured by your inferno and a new world will be created for you from the ashes. You can create anything in this life; I won't let you forget it.

CELESTITE

ELEMENT	AFFIRMATION
air	*I allow myself to rest and feel peace.*

CHAKRAS	LOCATIONS
third eye, crown	Madagascar, United States

MOHS HARDNESS	PAIRS WELL WITH
3–3.5	aquamarine, blue calcite, selenite

I prefer the quiet moments, the stillness of deep thoughts, the divine force of prayer. I whisper calming thoughts to you when you lay your head down to rest. I know you want to feel at peace; it's normal and healthy to want to live a harmonious life, a life without interruptions that cause you stress and sling your life into disarray. It's those situations that make the calming seasons of your life so cherished.

Keep me by your bedside when you crave the comfort of a friend. I'm here for you; tell me what's on your mind. I can help you to express the feelings you have resisted letting out. Your angels will hear you. When you hold me close know that I am working hard to fill your surroundings with the quiet, peaceful energy you deserve.

CHAROITE

ELEMENT	AFFIRMATION
air	*When I invest in myself I invest in everyone I love.*

CHAKRAS	LOCATION
crown, third eye, solar plexus	Russia

MOHS HARDNESS	PAIRS WELL WITH
5–6	amethyst, iolite, labradorite

I am the crystal of the violet ray. My purple haze forms a powerful protective energy shield around you that blocks out unwanted energies from messing with your flow. I value the art of treating yourself like royalty while also being good to those around you. I remind you to make service to your community a priority.

I want you to work on your own personal development, to expand your consciousness and focus on your spiritual path. When you're focused on your spirituality you'll soon come to realise that service to those around you also benefits you. When you and I combine our power you will feel a swarming of magic. As the energy builds your inspiration, intuition and dreams will unfold, leaving you feeling elevated and boundless.

CITRINE

ELEMENT	AFFIRMATION
fire △	*I am a magnet for abundance.*

CHARKAS	LOCATIONS
solar plexus, sacral, root	Brazil, Congo, Madagascar

MOHS HARDNESS	PAIRS WELL WITH
7	carnelian, pyrite, rutile, sunstone

I am the crystal mentor to manifesters and happiness hunters. Empowerment and expansion are my gifts to the world. When you hold me in your hands the energy I harness will radiate around you like sun rays hitting your face on a perfect summer day. I bring cheer into your life, enhancing your spirit with positivity.

I am like a battery jump-start to the creative energy that is already present inside you. When you need a boost, carry me and I will support you as you create an incredible life for yourself. I encourage you to transform the energy you channel into embodied reality in the physical world. With me by your side you will alchemise crystal magic into abundance and prosperity. The world is at your fingertips.

Did you know? Most citrine sold commercially is actually heated amethyst, as naturally occurring citrine is a lot rarer than it was once thought to be. To keep up with demand miners began heating amethyst to imitate the conditions that create natural citrine.

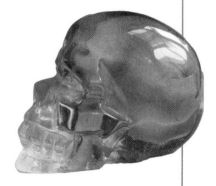

CLEAR QUARTZ

ELEMENTS	AFFIRMATION
all elements	*I amplify my intentions with crystal-clear focus.*

CHAKRAS	LOCATIONS
all chakras	all over the world

MOHS HARDNESS	PAIRS WELL WITH
7	all crystals

I am the crystal of infinite possibilities for charmed collectors seeking a trusted crystal companion. I sense your thoughts and intentions and magnify them. My incredible amplifying quality means that you can place me with any of your other crystal allies if you think they could use a little boost. I enhance their power and give them the endurance to emanate their healing vibrational frequencies for longer periods of time. Whether you're spellcasting, crystal gridding or meditating, I will transmute and enhance the energy in your space.

I ensure you maintain focus and a clear mind to allow for the best possible outcome for you. Carry me when you have low energy and you will be uplifted. I consider myself a jack of all trades, so let me know what you need help with and I will be there for you.

FIRE AGATE

ELEMENT fire △	**AFFIRMATION** *I can achieve anything I desire.*
CHAKRAS solar plexus, sacral, root	**LOCATIONS** Mexico, United States
MOHS HARDNESS 6-7	**PAIRS WELL WITH** carnelian, kyanite, pyrite

I am the crystal of burning desire for pilgrims who will stop at nothing on their quest for fulfilment. I am the crystal for those who seek inspiration and determination. Look deeply into my colours as they shimmer and sparkle like the fiery reflections of dragon scales. Like a dragon, I possess the powers of strength, success, wealth and magic. Allow my energy to set ablaze the hope and belief in your heart that you can achieve all that you set out to achieve.

As you gaze into my fire you will be ignited by your curiosity and creativity. Do you see all the potential pathways that lie ahead of you? Whichever path you choose, follow that path knowing that you are exactly where you are meant to be. You are on the road to greatness.

FLUORITE

ELEMENT
water ▽

AFFIRMATION
I am fearless and focused.

CHAKRAS
third eye, heart

LOCATIONS
Brazil, China, Madagascar, United States

MOHS HARDNESS
4

PAIRS WELL WITH
lapis lazuli, smoky quartz, sodalite

I am the crystal of the student, and my gift is that of clear thinking. When focus is of the utmost importance, come to me and I will sharpen your mind. If you have been called to work with me you may need help clearing away mental clutter that is fogging your concentration or decision-making processes. I will help you to remember what's important and help you to let go of the noise that causes mental confusion.

I clarify and stabilise your energy field so you can move through challenges without the influence of negative energy and stress. My calming energy and razor-sharp focus make me a formidable ally when you are ready to step out of fear and into a new chapter of your life.

GARNET

ELEMENT	AFFIRMATION
earth ▽	*I am at peace with where I am.*

CHACRA	LOCATIONS
root	Australia, Brazil, United States

MOHS HARDNESS	PAIRS WELL WITH
6.5–7.5	bloodstone, hematite, ruby fuchsite

I want you to bring your focus back into the present moment, to feel the breeze against your skin and hear the birds chirping outside. This big wonderful world can feel overwhelming sometimes, and I am here to keep you grounded and help you find your centre.

Turn to me when you feel the world is demanding and you're falling behind, barely achieving or not working hard enough. There is no shame in taking pause, listening to your body and resting when you need rest. There is strength in overcoming your insecurities and finding peace within yourself exactly where you are right now: not in your fantasised future, not when you reach your goal, not when you look your best but right now in the present moment. These are the lessons I wish to pass on to you.

HEMATITE

ELEMENT	AFFIRMATION
earth ▽	*I remain grounded while I integrate my spiritual lessons.*

CHAKRA	LOCATIONS
root	Australia, Brazil, China, Morocco

MOHS HARDNESS	PAIRS WELL WITH
5.5–6.5	bloodstone, mookaite jasper, red jasper

I am the crystal of duality and actualisation. I will teach you to appreciate the beauty of the human experience in all its glory, heaviness and mundanity. It's important to find the balance between seeking spiritual enlightenment and appreciating your time here in this fragile human form. When I am near you will find it is much easier to integrate the spiritual lessons you have learned into your everyday life.

I bring you a deeper and more meaningful connection to this earthly plane. I aim to help you find your ground and cultivate a profound sense of security and safety in your being. With my help your plans and ideas will be realised into your physical world, as though you merely plucked it out of your mind's eye and planted it in the soil before your feet. Now it's time to watch it all unfold.

HOWLITE

ELEMENT
air

AFFIRMATION
I release negativity with every exhale and breathe in positivity.

CHAKRA
crown

LOCATION
United States

MOHS HARDNESS
3.5

PAIRS WELL WITH
aventurine, labradorite, ocean jasper

I am a calming presence, determined to keep your mind at ease. There's no need to stress when I am with you. Let your noisy thoughts be calm; let your anger wash away. I will teach you to let go. Don't hold on to the pain. Trust me, you'll feel so much better. You'll sleep better too! Be patient with yourself and with others.

I see the positive ray of light inside you, and if you spend enough time with me you'll see it too.

IOLITE

ELEMENT	AFFIRMATION
air	*I open my mind to conscious expansion.*

CHAKRA	LOCATIONS
third eye	Brazil, India, Madagascar

MOHS HARDNESS	PAIRS WELL WITH
7–7.5	azurite, lapis lazuli, turquoise

I am the crystal of the visionary, the ally to the creative spirit who seeks to explore the innermost areas of their imagination and mind. I enhance your capacity to express these discoveries through your creativity, whether that be in life, work, art or anything else. I will take you on a voyage through time and space, pursuing answers about your origins, past lives and soul purpose.

I expand your awareness and open your mind to visions from beyond. Like a million little lights turning on in the distance, suddenly you will see so much more, you will see what has always been there waiting for you to open your eyes to it. Messages from your angels and guides will be clearer now if you are willing to hear them.

JADE

ELEMENT	AFFIRMATION
earth ▽	*I am happy, healthy and fulfilled.*

CHAKRA	LOCATIONS
heart	Burma, China, New Zealand

MOHS HARDNESS	PAIRS WELL WITH
6–7	hematite, prehnite, turquoise

I carry with me ancient and sacred energy that I've spread across the world for centuries. I enhance your life-force energy. It pulses through your body, giving you zest for movement, the will to breathe and strength and vitality so you may create a life of fulfilment. This force enables your entire existence.

I will nourish you with an ever-flowing harmony, keeping your energy in balance and alignment. I am healing and love all in one. Hold me and feel your heart's expansion. Allow the feeling of unconditional love to fill you and ground you into total bliss. When you improve your auric and spiritual health a cascade effect will enable your physical and emotional health to also be at their optimum.

KUNZITE

ELEMENT
water

AFFIRMATION
I give myself permission to heal.

CHAKRA
heart

LOCATIONS
Afghanistan, Pakistan

MOHS HARDNESS
6.5–7

PAIRS WELL WITH
malachite, pink tourmaline, rhodochrosite

I am the crystal of transcendent love, a messenger to those who wish to embark on an expedition to emotional reconstruction. Do you remember what it felt like to be a spirit soaring through the infinite, connected to all, filled with divine love, to have unlimited space in your heart for yourself and all of those you hold dear?

Allow my gentle essence to wash over you. Feel the calmness and surrender as I whisper to you 'Let it all go: I give you permission to release this heaviness' – the density that blocks the entrance to the space that once flowed so freely with affection and appreciation. I remind you to send this heaviness back home. Send it with love and give it thanks, for it served its purpose and left you with the lessons and compassion you needed to prepare for a heart-alignment renovation.

KYANITE

ELEMENTS	AFFIRMATION
all elements	*I am the conscious expression of the universe.*

CHAKRAS	LOCATIONS
all chakras	Brazil, Mexico, South Africa

MOHS HARDNESS	PAIRS WELL WITH
4.5–7	azurite, clear quartz, iolite

I invite you to embark on a mystical odyssey into the dream world, to explore the astral realms and expand your awareness to all that is possible beyond your touch and sight. Hold me over your brow and feel the doors to your intuition crack open. You are a psychic being whose gifts wait for you to invite them into your life.

I am the crystal of connection, a bridge between your mind and the minds of those around you. Like an electric charge, your cognisance is switched on and transmitted to the ultimate receiver, the collective consciousness, the universe. You are magic. I am a spiral of energy coursing through you, clearing the blockages in your chakras and guiding you to express all that you're experiencing with truth and clarity.

LABRADORITE

ELEMENT	AFFIRMATION
air	*I trust my gifts and control where my energy is spent.*

CHAKRAS	LOCATIONS
all chakras	Madagascar, Canada

MOHS HARDNESS	PAIRS WELL WITH
6-6.5	charoite, moonstone, shungite

I am the crystal of transformation. Carry me when you need reminding that you are a unique and gifted soul, a one of a kind spirit. I'll help you to connect with your innate intuitive knowledge. Whether you have strong gut feelings, predict things that you can't explain in your dreams or see spirits beyond the veil, spending time with me will help you to attune to and trust your gifts. No more second-guessing!

Using these gifts can take up quite a lot of energy, so you'll be drawn to me when you're experiencing transformation in your life. If you're feeling spent from your day-to-day grind, from other people draining you or from working your magic, know that I am here for you. I will help to regulate your energy levels by shielding you so you don't feel zapped by the end of the day.

LAPIS LAZULI

ELEMENT	AFFIRMATION
air	*I connect to my intuition with ease and express myself authentically.*

CHAKRAS	LOCATIONS
third eye, throat	Afghanistan, Chile

MOHS HARDNESS	PAIRS WELL WITH
5–5.5	blue lace agate, moonstone, sodalite

I instil in you the gift of prophecy, the ability to see the future before you. Listen to the wind: she is guiding you toward your highest purpose, to the truth you have always known deep within, to the faith that has motivated you in all your decisions and every step of the way as you inch closer and closer to the divinely inspired destination ahead.

Hold me and you will connect to the counsel of the pharaohs and mystics long passed, whose spirits are joined by my royal blue radiance. Their influence navigates you to live your life with integrity and dignity. Honour me by utilising the wisdom I have bestowed upon you, always expressing yourself with honesty and authenticity.

LARIMAR

ELEMENT	AFFIRMATION
water ▽	*I am powerful when I explore what makes me feel vulnerable.*

CHAKRA	LOCATION
throat	Dominican Republic

MOHS HARDNESS	PAIRS WELL WITH
4.5–5	aquamarine, blue calcite, ocean jasper

I envelop you in my serene radiance and welcome you with loving arms. Do you feel it radiating from me? Allow my softening energy to surround you and lead you to your own gentle nature. See it for what it is: a superpower. I can see it within you. Understand that it takes great strength to be gentle and have pride in knowing that you can be the master of your own temperament.

You need a safe place to feel at peace, to rest your mind and spill your words. I can be that place for you. Tender soul, I am the hidden treasure formed in the crevices between a volcano and the Caribbean Sea. I am a fusion of fire and water, a symbol of my ability to help you navigate and calm even the most powerful and eruptive of your feelings. Ride the emotional wave, allowing it to transmute through you, and I will guide you, renewed, safely to shore.

LEPIDOLITE

ELEMENT
water ▽

AFFIRMATION
I change what I can and accept what I cannot.

CHAKRAS
heart, third eye

LOCATIONS
Brazil, Madagascar

MOHS HARDNESS
2.5–3

PAIRS WELL WITH
amazonite, fluorite, smoky quartz

Dear friend, I will sit by your side and listen when your worries are raining down on you, splashing one by one and creating puddles of doubt around you. I will be your bridge to the place where woes only stay for long enough to help you see more clearly. I will whisper to you: 'You can't control everything, but you have the choice to accept or walk away.'

Allow your mind to release your anxieties. I want you to feel at ease, like you are floating down a stream on a beautiful spring day, breathing in the warmth of the sun or drifting into a peaceful sleep. Dear friend, you can let it all go when I am here.

MALACHITE

ELEMENT		AFFIRMATION
fire △		*I am fuelled by the powerful force of love.*

CHAKRAS		LOCATIONS
solar plexus, heart		Australia, Congo, Morocco, Namibia

MOHS HARDNESS	PAIRS WELL WITH
3.5–4	rhodonite, rose quartz, tiger's eye

I want you to know with every fibre of your being that you are strong and resilient and fuelled by the powerful force of love. With my help you will steer your mind from the thoughts and intentions of others and instead focus on your own hopes and dreams. Allow me to focus on keeping you safe from the energies of those who might wish you harm.

Know this: you can stand in your power without standing on someone else's neck. Stand in your power with humility and have courage! I will help you by purifying you of the emotional scars that are left behind from the past. I will guide you to take action on finding the path that aligns with your divine life purpose.

MOOKAITE JASPER

ELEMENT	AFFIRMATION
earth ▽	*My ancestors will guide me when I call to them.*

CHAKRAS	LOCATION
solar plexus, sacral, root	Australia

MOHS HARDNESS	PAIRS WELL WITH
7	opal, shungite, turquoise

I am the soil, the sun and the stars unified in a crystalline form. When you hold me near you will be imbued with an unstoppable willpower, a hunger and determination you have never felt before. I remind you that you are governed only by your own free will. Should you need the support of your ancestors before you, call to them and they will be with you. With my help you can access your ancestral wisdom.

I am a gift to you from the earth; I am medicine for your spirit. Hold me and feel your feet rooted deeply into the dirt below you, syncing you to the earth's natural rhythm and clearing your soul of ancient karmic debris.

MOONSTONE

ELEMENT	AFFIRMATION
air △	*I step into the unknown with courage.*

CHAKRAS	LOCATIONS
crown, third eye	Burma, India

MOHS HARDNESS	PAIRS WELL WITH
6–6.5	kunzite, lepidolite, rutile

I am the crystal that honours the waxing and waning nature of life. Just as the moon moves through cycles, so do you. I facilitate a seamless transition when you are nearing the end of a phase. In turn, I remind you to celebrate and acknowledge that the ending of one period in your life marks the beginning of something new. Infinite possibilities lie ahead of you, and although stepping into the unknown can be scary you should know that my energetic protection is here to support you the whole way through.

I am the crystal of divine goddess energy. I am here to remind you that you're capable of connecting to a powerful creative and cleansing force, a force that will drive you to identify what in your life must be released in order to make space for your rebirth.

OBSIDIAN

ELEMENT		AFFIRMATION
earth ▽		*I take ownership of my actions.*

CHAKRA		LOCATIONS
root		Mexico, United States

MOHS HARDNESS	PAIRS WELL WITH
5.5	black tourmaline, garnet, red jasper

Mirror, mirror on the wall: who's the least self-aware of all? I am not here to gently sway you; I am not here to hold your hand through hard times. What I am here for is results, and I will waste no time in getting them. Look into my volcanic glass surface and feel all of the repressed garbage you've been avoiding bubbling up and erupting from you. Let it all out.

You can't move on from something if you're not willing to look at it and address it. Whether it's something that was done to you or something you've done to yourself or someone else, if you've been called to work with me it means it's time to face the music. Own your shortcomings and the emotions that are holding you back; it's time to deal with them. One thing I can promise you is that although it won't be easy, you'll feel much lighter when this is done. I am a protector, after all, and the best way I can protect you is to teach you how to protect yourself.

OCEAN JASPER

ELEMENT	AFFIRMATION
earth ▽	*I am in control of my emotions; my emotions are not in control of me.*

CHAKRAS	LOCATION
throat, heart, solar plexus	Madagascar

MOHS HARDNESS	PAIRS WELL WITH
7	howlite, lepidolite, unakite

You might feel drawn to me when you're having a hard time connecting to your feelings. You may feel called to me when you're drowning in your emotions and there's no life float in sight. I want you to ride the wave of my energy to emotional growth. I will help you learn to cope with the full spectrum of your feelings and in the end you will feel empowered.

Have hope and know that with me navigating you will be in control of your emotions, not the other way around. Open your heart and have compassion for yourself and for others. I remind you to have patience and understanding. It's important to honour the fact that you will move through your lessons and grow at your own pace.

OPAL

ELEMENTS	AFFIRMATION
all elements	*I attract all that I desire with ease and joy.*

CHAKRAS	LOCATIONS
all chakras	Australia, Ethiopia, Mexico, United States

MOHS HARDNESS	PAIRS WELL WITH
5.5–6.5	citrine, fire agate, rutile, sunstone

I might not be a genie but I'm here to grant your wishes. You know the rules, though, right? I'm going to need you to be very specific. I bring wonder and magic into your life. I am fun and adventurous and full of life and always looking to change things up. I can sense what you're thinking about and, like a magnet, I'll pull that right into your life. It's a good idea to keep those thoughts focused on positive things because I am the ultimate cheerleader and I will be amplifying your intentions so the universe can hear you loud and clear!

I am the crystal of colours, a prism that refracts light in all directions. When you carry me with you you carry a light everywhere you go, a light that illuminates even the darkest of times.

PINK
TOURMALINE

ELEMENT	AFFIRMATION
water ▽	*I open my heart to free-flowing and abundant love.*

CHARKA		LOCATIONS
heart		Afghanistan, Brazil, Madagascar, Pakistan, United States

MOHS HARDNESS	PAIRS WELL WITH
7–7.5	kunzite, rhodochrosite, rose quartz

I am a calming crystal, emanating a loving vibrational frequency to soothe your emotional state. When you feel off balance and need a nurturing influence to help regulate your nerves, allow my warm energy to wash over you. I will help you to stay stress free.

I encourage you to connect with your gentle side, which will help you to be a more tolerant and understanding person towards others and yourself. Emotional healing begins in your heart. When you feel called to me, hold me near and my energy will radiate deep into your heart centre, clearing away blockages that prevent you from opening yourself up to sharing or accepting free-flowing love.

PREHNITE

ELEMENTS
water,
earth

AFFIRMATION
I love and accept myself for who I am.

CHAKRAS
heart, solar plexus

LOCATIONS
Australia, Namibia

MOHS HARDNESS
6–6.5

PAIRS WELL WITH
jade, malachite, shungite

The energy of the forest dwells within me, awaiting invitation into your life. I am the crystal of the trees, mountains and valleys; you will feel called to me when your spirit yearns for the tranquillity of being in nature. Allow my gentle energy to embrace you and draw roots from within you, grounding you and leaving you feeling nurtured by Gaia. Hold me close when the chaos of the modern world leaves you feeling disconnected from the rhythm of the earth.

I encourage you to look within. Come to me when you need support with recognising and processing your vast range of emotions. With my guidance you will learn to break down the emotional barriers that prevent you from seeing your own self-worth.

PYRITE

ELEMENT
earth

AFFIRMATION
My focus and determination are unwavering.

CHAKRA
solar plexus

LOCATIONS
Italy, Peru, Russia, Spain

MOHS HARDNESS
6–6.5

PAIRS WELL WITH
citrine, hematite, rutile

I am the crystal of ambition. My power will appeal to you when you seek to achieve an intimidating goal or manifest some greatness into your life. Call on me when you find yourself feeling stuck, idle or apathetic. I will reignite your determination and break through the stagnant energy that is blocking your creative thinking and confidence. I bestow on you energies that strengthen your spirit and give you the tenacity and endurance to persevere.

Manifesting requires an immense amount of energy and willpower, and you will feel called to me when you require some help with staying the path. I am the crystal of getting things done. With me by your side nothing can slow you down or distract you from the inspiring path ahead.

RED JASPER

ELEMENT	AFFIRMATION
earth ▽	*I believe in myself; I will never give up!*

CHARKAS		LOCATIONS
sacral, root		Brazil, India, United States

MOHS HARDNESS	PAIRS WELL WITH
6.5–7	fire agate, pyrite, tiger's eye

I am the crystal of courage for souls who need to kick-start their journey towards healing energetic blockages around their adequacy. Hold me close and know that you will be fortified with bravery and determination. I remind you to keep pushing forward one step at a time when your path ahead seems like a never-ending uphill battle. You must believe in yourself! I will not let you give up.

You are a creative soul made of the earth and stars. Remember who you are; remember your interconnection with the divine and all that exists in this universe. Your potential is limitless; your mark on this world is eternal. I am an ever-flowing source of energy, emanating inspiration for you to utilise and to show you that you have more to offer than you may have ever realised.

RHODOCHROSITE

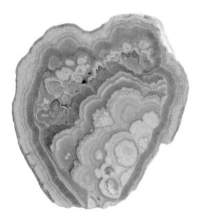

ELEMENT	AFFIRMATION
fire △	*I honour and love myself without reservation.*

CHAKRAS	LOCATIONS
heart, solar plexus	Argentina, Peru

MOHS HARDNESS	PAIRS WELL WITH
3.5–4	kunzite, pink tourmaline, rhodonite, rose quartz

I will energise your spirit with love and lift up your heart when you need to be nurtured. I am the crystal of compassion for those who seek a kind and loving embrace for a heavy soul. You will feel drawn to me when you recognise in yourself that you must place more emphasis on self-love. I remind you of the importance of honouring your emotions and caring for yourself wholeheartedly, without reservation or hesitation.

My energy will grow within you, guiding you to devote this compassion to those around you as well as to yourself. My hope is that when I am near you will feel a sense of relief and ease and be comforted by my radiant warmth.

RHODONITE

ELEMENTS
earth, fire

AFFIRMATION
I open my heart to others and share my love generously.

CHAKRAS
heart, root

LOCATIONS
Australia, Madagascar, United States

MOHS HARDNESS
5.5–6

PAIRS WELL WITH
prehnite, rose quartz, ruby fuchsite

My gift to you is a simple gift but arguably the greatest one of all: love. Love is a powerful force that has the potential to change the world. You will be called to me when you require your heart to open and expand. My energy will surround you and compel you to share your love with generosity, which will benefit not only you but also those around you. When you have love in your heart you will be kinder and more patient and forgiving.

I am a stone of passion that cannot be extinguished. This passionate energy rises from the earth and regenerates you. It will drive your determination and sense of self-worth. When you are good to others you will feel good about yourself. This is the lesson I wish to impart to you.

ROSE QUARTZ

ELEMENT	AFFIRMATION
air	*My soul is revived by the powerful force of love.*

CHAKRA	LOCATIONS
heart	Brazil, Madagascar

MOHS HARDNESS	PAIRS WELL WITH
7	pink tourmaline, rhodochrosite, selenite

Let your heart shine through! Feel the expansion of your entire being as you hold me near and breathe me in. Melt into my comforting and nurturing energies, allowing them to flow into your life. I am the crystalline embodiment of love; I am the light; I am the smell before rain, the stars in the sky, beauty and bliss. I am love.

Although my influence will certainly open your life to more loving encounters, I am not here merely to play cupid. Love is the highest vibrational frequency, shifting the energy of all spaces and things. Stagnant and discordant energy must shift in the presence of love, and all negativity must be eliminated. I revive the heartbeat of all spaces. Do not underestimate love, or me.

RUBY FUCHSITE

ELEMENT	AFFIRMATION
water ▽	*I honour myself by prioritising my needs.*

CHAKRAS	LOCATIONS
heart, root	India, Pakistan

MOHS HARDNESS	PAIRS WELL WITH
ruby 9, fuchsite 3	garnet, jade, red jasper, unakite

I am the crystal of deep introspection. I help you to form a union between your deepest desires and your physical reality. What is the void in your life you aren't recognising? You will be called to me when you need to find the courage to step into the unknown. I remind you to honour yourself by taking action on your wants and needs.

Do not shy away from your empowerment: step into it. I am here for you, to encourage you to look deep within yourself and acknowledge what makes you an individual. Learning to value your unique traits will bring you closer to manifesting your dreams.

RUTILE

ELEMENTS all elements	**AFFIRMATION** *I am ready to step into my power and towards my destiny.*
CHAKRAS all chakras	**LOCATIONS** China, Brazil, United States
MOHS HARDNESS 7	**PAIRS WELL WITH** carnelian, citrine, pyrite

I am the crystal of quickening for the inspired mind who wishes to manifest and achieve their dreams at lightning speed. I open up your psychic channels so you may be divinely guided by your intuition and messages from spirit. I am an energetic echo, amplifying your deep desires so they may reverberate out into the universe for long after you've set the intention.

When you work with me you will feel expansion as you emanate a constant flowing of energy from your whole being, activating and assisting your ability to attract your goals. I wish to see you transform your life, to step into your power and into the life you're destined to live. You will be drawn to me when you are ready for this change.

SELENITE

ELEMENT	AFFIRMATION
air △	*I am protected and purified by divine light frequency.*

CHAKRAS	LOCATIONS
third eye, crown	Australia, Mexico, Morocco, United States

MOHS HARDNESS	PAIRS WELL WITH
2	amethyst, celestite, rose quartz

I am the crystal of divine light frequency, a celestial frequency connecting to angelic realms that open your soul to spiritual expansion. My quest is to awaken your higher energy centres so I may serve as a conduit for angelic communication and deepen your connection to the divine. I am gentle and powerful; purifying and nurturing. I am a protector, driven by the force of light, ensuring all people and spaces are cleansed and enlightened so that no dark energies feel welcome to dwell.

Hold me near and invoke tranquillity into your life. As my gentle energies sweep through the energetic dust and debris like a feather, trust that you will feel a quiet peace. You will be called to me when you need blockages in your body's energy field or your home to be dissolved and transmuted.

Tip: store your other crystals with your selenite to keep them cleansed. Its purifying energy will speed along your other crystals' natural ability to stabilise their energy.

SHUNGITE

ELEMENTS	AFFIRMATION
all elements	*I am connected to all of nature's power and potential.*

CHAKRAS	LOCATION
all chakras	Russia

MOHS HARDNESS	PAIRS WELL WITH
3.5–4	jade, mookaite jasper, selenite

I am the stone of detoxification, both physically and energetically. My carbon form might not shimmer like some of my crystalline friends, but don't be disillusioned and think I am not filled with the magic of the earth. I was formed in ancient river waters long before your ancestors ever placed their feet on soil. I carry the elements of earth, air, water and fire with me, connecting you to all of nature's power and potential.

I emanate harmonious centring energy, redirecting feelings of chaos or stress and purifying inharmonious energy into a state of calm and collection. Whether that be the noisy energetic static of electromagnetic waves or toxic waste floating down a river stream, I will absorb and transform it. All life on earth is made of carbon, and so am I. With the power of the elements you can transform, metamorphose, re-imagine and recreate the energy in your life.

SMOKY QUARTZ

ELEMENT	AFFIRMATION
earth ▽	*My worth is not defined by my productivity.*

CHAKRA	LOCATIONS
root	Australia, Brazil, Madagascar, South Africa

MOHS HARDNESS	PAIRS WELL WITH
7	black tourmaline, fluorite, garnet, lepidolite

I know that you may sometimes feel the worries in your life are overpowering you. If you have heard my call, I'm offering you my grounding comfort. Lean on me: I am here to help keep your mind at ease. Do you ever feel so stressed that all rationality seems to dissipate from your consciousness? Do not be swallowed up by this overwhelm!

Come to me and I will bring you back to reality. I will help you to focus your thoughts into productive and balanced thinking. I will collect your confusion, worries and fears and plant them deep into the earth like seeds so they may be reborn and blossom into something new.

SODALITE

ELEMENT
air

AFFIRMATION
I open my mind to the mysteries of the universe.

CHAKRA
third eye

LOCATIONS
Brazil, Namibia, United States

MOHS HARDNESS
5.5–6

PAIRS WELL WITH
azurite, fluorite, iolite

I am the crystal of mental and intuitive acuity. I enable you to tap into your psychic senses, enhancing your accuracy with spiritual divination, tarot readings and channelling. I am a laser focus for your mental capacity, perfecting the clarity of your thoughts and accessing the inner wisdom yet unchartered deep within.

Are you developing your spiritual practice or do you require a little booster while you explore the many avenues of spirituality? I support the expansion of your mind in all areas, including your grasp of the unknown and the divine. As you branch your consciousness beyond the mainstream teachings and understanding of the world around you, hold me near and know that your studies will be in depth and inspiring.

SUNSTONE

ELEMENT	AFFIRMATION
fire △	*I embrace the radiant light surrounding me.*

CHAKRAS	LOCATIONS
solar plexus, sacral	India, Norway, United States

MOHS HARDNESS	PAIRS WELL WITH
6–6.5	citrine, jade, tiger's eye

I am the stone of the sun, shimmering brightly and bouncing my radiant light around you so I may brighten your day. I am a radiant glimmer of hope on days when things aren't going your way. Whether you're feeling happy or blue, I'll bring more joy to you! Be energised by my warm embrace. Just as the sun gives energy to all life on this beautiful planet, I am a constant source of fuel for your spirit and the energy that surrounds you.

I invite blessings into your life so you may move through it with ease and excitement. I am a power bank for your creative and empowerment energy centres. Come to me when you need a boost in confidence or a reminder that you, too, are a radiant light shining your brilliance into the world.

TIGER'S EYE

ELEMENTS
fire,
earth

AFFIRMATION
I pounce on opportunities with courage and determination.

CHAKRAS
solar plexus,
sacral, root

LOCATIONS
Australia, Brazil, South Africa,
United States

MOHS HARDNESS
6.5–7

PAIRS WELL WITH
fire agate, garnet, pyrite

I am the crystal of the eye of the tiger. You have been led to work with me, so now is your time to step into your inner animalistic and primal being. You are called to embody the relentless and determined spirit of the tiger.

Keep your eye on the prize. You must be tactful and never give up. Your will is your power, and with me near there is nothing that can distract you from your determination to succeed. I may come across as intense, but I am here to train you and to build confidence within you. I am here to ensure you will never be without the courage required to step into your power again! Be brave and you will be rewarded.

TURQUOISE

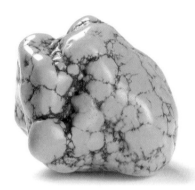

ELEMENTS	AFFIRMATION
all elements	*I am connected to and express my wisdom from lifetimes passed.*

CHARKA		LOCATIONS
throat		Africa, China, Iran, Mexico, United States

MOHS HARDNESS	PAIRS WELL WITH
5–6	lapis lazuli, mookaite jasper, obsidian

Have you been called to work with me; were you drawn into my blue ray of energy? I am an old soul in the crystal kingdom and I have plenty of wisdom to give, and I know you do as well. Take some time to centre yourself and think sensibly about your words before they depart your lips. You're a wise soul with lifetimes of knowledge stored in the cells of your being. I encourage you to express this wisdom and all other thoughts and feelings you may be experiencing.

I am the crystal of balance; find comfort in my presence when you need a crystal friend to help bring security to your life. This balancing energy grants you protection from outside energetic influence and also protection from your own self-sabotaging habits. Allow my grounding energy to bring you to a place of peace and strength.

UNAKITE

ELEMENT	AFFIRMATION
earth ▽	*I open myself to a life of stability and grounded love.*

CHARKA	LOCATIONS
heart	Australia, United States

MOHS HARDNESS	PAIRS WELL WITH
6.5–7	amazonite, rhodonite, ruby fuchsite

I am the crystal of grounded love. Are you showing up for the people you love, for yourself? How are you sharing the love you have for those who deserve it the most and, more importantly, who are you focusing your love on who hasn't earned or deserved it?

To be loved is a beautiful thing, so open your heart to it. Not to a crush or a fling, but to something real. Open up to a solid foundation of caring stability, patience and reliability. I release the bad habits that impair your judgement about where you place the energy of your heart. I encourage you to look at your relationships and work towards connections that support a sense of balance and well-being within you.

APPENDIX I:

COMMONLY ASKED QUESTIONS

When people begin their crystal journey they usually have a lot of questions, and there's a lot to learn about these seemingly mysterious rocks. This appendix contains some of the more common questions I have been asked over the years, and I hope the answers will enhance your journey with crystals and demystify crystal healing for you. Ultimately, I want crystal healing to be accessible to you and for you to discover that crystal healing is not as daunting or complex as it might first appear.

WHAT DO I DO WITH THEM?

Display your crystals: there is absolutely nothing wrong with collecting crystals to display in your home and simply allowing them to enhance the energy of your space. If this is as far as you want to take crystal healing that is totally fine. Carry your crystals with you: many people find comfort in having their smaller crystals in their pockets throughout the day or even tucked into their bra. Meditate with your crystals: if you have a frequent meditation practice, try enhancing it by holding on to a crystal throughout your meditation.

WHY AM I DRAWN TO THE SAME CRYSTAL ALL THE TIME?

When you find yourself constantly drawn to the same crystal over and over again it's usually an indication that that particular crystal would be beneficial for you at that time. Your energetic needs constantly change depending on what you are going through in life, the thoughts you are harbouring and the emotions you are experiencing. Your energy is also influenced by the foods you eat, the people you spend time with and how active you are. Just as you might crave a certain food when you have a mineral deficiency, you will be drawn to a crystal when you have an energetic deficiency. Trust your gut feeling and embrace your crystal craving!

You'll know that a crystal can benefit you when you find yourself frequently drawn to it.

WHY DO SOME CRYSTALS MAKE ME FEEL UNCOMFORTABLE?

Sometimes you just won't vibe with a particular crystal, and that's okay. Maybe you aren't attracted to it because of its appearance, and while some might consider that crystal blasphemy to each their own: we don't all have the same taste. If you find that some crystals make you feel physically or energetically uncomfortable it's likely there is a significant energetic shift happening within your body that you are not ready for or need to happen in a more gentle way. You may decide to avoid that mineral and seek your crystal healing from stones that make you feel supported. If you do decide to embrace the discomfort I suggest working with the stone that makes you feel uncomfortable for short periods of time and incrementally lengthening the time you sit with that stone. You may find that it becomes your favourite crystal in the end.

WHY DO MY CRYSTALS SOMETIMES BREAK?

At some point along your crystal journey you will have broken a crystal, and you may stop to wonder whether it was a case of bad luck or whether it had some sort of spiritual significance. There could be a number of reasons for why a crystal breaks; there are no hard and fast rules when it comes to crystal healing. While sometimes it might just mean that you've accidentally dropped your favourite crystal point onto your tiled floor, I tend to think everything happens for a reason.

The ride or die crystal: the most commonly adopted philosophy is that a broken crystal signifies the crystal has absorbed negative energy surrounding you in order to protect you. It's the crystal-healing equivalent of taking a bullet for someone! The idea is that the crystal has sacrificed itself in order to prevent any harm coming to you.

The training wheels crystal: think about what was happening in your life when you decided to work with this particular crystal. Often crystals break when the cycle of your life it was supporting you through has come to an end. It can sometimes be the crystal's way of saying 'You don't need me any more; you've got this!' If this rings true to you it is likely the cause of the crystal breaking.

The sharing is caring crystal: some people believe that when a crystal breaks the universe is telling them there is someone in their life waiting to share in that crystal's energy. The next time you break a crystal, consider gifting it to someone you know who can benefit from its unique healing properties.

There are a number of different approaches you can take to broken crystals that will bring you closure and also honour the crystal for the part it has played in your life.

Repair: if your crystal has a clean break it can be repaired with a clear superglue or epoxy. In fact, in the gemstone industry there are many crystals that are repaired with glue when they are cut, carved or

set in jewellery before they are sold on to retailers and then consumers. Repairing is typically reserved for harder crystals (a Mohs hardness of more than 5), as softer crystals may not respond well to glues. If you choose to repair your crystal give it a good cleanse before working with it again.

Return: what goes up must come down, as within so without. Crystals live their lives and then break, a death of sorts; such is the cycle of life. The breaking of a crystal signifies life, death and rebirth, so when a crystal breaks you can pay homage to its impact on your life by returning it to the earth in a commemorative way by, for example, burying it in the earth or placing it in the sea, where it will be reborn as it becomes a part of its new environment. Whichever method you choose, take a moment to give thanks to the crystal.

Ration: when a crystal breaks you will be left with multiple crystals that previously made up one whole piece. While some people may choose to deal with their broken crystals in other ways, there is nothing wrong with continuing to enjoy and appreciate the beauty and gifts of your crystal if that is what you feel drawn to do. Consider sharing the crystal remnants with your friends and loved ones, or scatter the broken pieces among your house plants or garden. Continuing to love your crystals after they have broken is a testament to your ability to accept and appreciate the impermanence and imperfections of life.

HOW CAN CRYSTALS IMPROVE MY LIFE?

Living a holistic life means understanding that everything is intrinsically linked: mind, body and soul. Health and beauty begin with a foundation of clear energy, so if you don't care for yourself on spiritual, energetic or emotional levels the unresolved blockages will eventually manifest into your physical body. The energy has to go somewhere. This is accepted philosophy in traditional Chinese medicine and in healing modalities such as kinesiology, so why do so many people have a hard time accepting the benefits of crystals? It can be hard to accept something that has been labelled 'woo-woo' for such a long time.

Everything holds vibrational frequency; this is scientifically known and accepted. Think of it this way: all crystals emanate unique

Crystals hold a vibrational frequency you can attune to.

vibrational frequencies depending on their colour, crystal structure, size and so on. People also emanate unique vibrational frequencies depending on their thoughts, emotional states and health. When you hold crystals you are able to attune to them and allow their frequencies to influence or elevate your own vibe.

219

ARE RARE STONES NECESSARY FOR SPIRITUAL GROWTH?

I can't deny the allure of rare and beautiful stones but, no, they are not at all necessary. Spiritual growth and crystal healing are not exclusively for the wealthy, so don't buy into the idea that you need expensive or rare stones to get a high vibe. One of the biggest misconceptions I've encountered as a crystal merchant is the notion that you need rare, expensive crystals to connect to high vibrational energy because only then will you begin your true ascension. This is utter rubbish. Energy healing, crystal healing, spiritual development and all other wonderfully magical-related avenues are for everyone to explore, not just the wealthy and privileged.

Even commonly found crystals hold enormous power.

The truth is you don't actually need to buy anything to find inner peace or connect to your psychic abilities. You don't need to buy anything to communicate with those beyond the veil or heal your emotional or spiritual bodies. Crystals are tools that aid in the healing work you are capable of doing all by yourself; however, when you work with crystals you will be offered a helping hand. In the same way that different foods offer different nutritional value, some overlapping, crystals offer energetic value and some crystals also overlap.

The universe is divinely perfect and was created with everything within it that you could ever need. If you can accept this as truth and feel in your heart with all of your knowing that this statement is accurate, then it makes sense that the crystals that are abundantly needed will be abundantly available. It makes sense that the job of assisting millions of people seeking crystal healing for various applications would not be left to a rare and hard-to-find mineral outside of the average person's budget. Let's throw that notion in the bin once and for all.

Whenever you are in doubt turn to clear quartz, which is so versatile in its use that you can use it as a replacement for just about any other crystal. Crystals are for everyone and you can achieve just as much with a clear quartz crystal and dedicated, focused intention as you can with any other rare, high-vibe crystal. In an ideal world we would all have access to highly sought rare crystals but that's not reality. The best magic is practical and accessible, so keep your quartz close by as it's your new best friend!

QUICK
CRYSTAL
METAPHYSICAL
GUIDE

Amazonite helps you to communicate your truth and process your emotions.

Amethyst aligns your mind, body and spirit, connecting you to your spirituality.

Aquamarine helps you to keep your cool and express yourself calmly.

Aventurine assists with heart expansion and maintaining a positive mental attitude.

Azurite encourages you to trust your intuition and embrace your psychic gifts.

Black tourmaline cleanses you of bad vibes and acts as a barrier to keep them out.

Bloodstone reminds you to set firm boundaries and believe in yourself.

Blue calcite allows you to tap into and express your ideas and inspiration.

Blue lace agate helps you to find your inner peace and speak with your angels.

Carnelian helps you to feel confident, courageous and creative.

Celestite brings peaceful energies into your life and home.

Charoite is a stone of spiritual expansion and protection.

Citrine is a crystal of joy that uplifts your spirit and aids in manifesting.

Clear quartz aids in mental clarity and will transmute energy to keep your vibes high.

Fire agate reminds you to pursue a path that leads to fulfilment.

Fluorite helps you to concentrate and make decisions; it is the stone of students.

Garnet.

Garnet emits a strong earth energy that keeps you feeling brave and grounded.

Hematite helps you to stay grounded while you integrate spiritual lessons.

Howlite eliminates anger and helps with sleep problems.

Iolite encourages expansion of your imagination and intuition.

Jade keeps your energy harmonised for overall health and well-being.

Kunzite helps you to connect to loving and caring energies.

Kyanite clears energetic debris that aids enhanced intuition.

Labradorite protects your energy and magically transforms your life.

Lapis lazuli helps you connect to your intuition and express yourself authentically.

Larimar shows you that there is strength in exploring your vulnerabilities.

Lepidolite teaches you to release anxiety and find acceptance.

Malachite empowers you to heal emotional wounds that block your personal growth.

Mookaite jasper releases you from karmic debris passed on from your ancestors.

Moonstone helps you to navigate new beginnings and release the past.

Obsidian encourages you to process repressed emotions, experiences and aspects of yourself.

Ocean jasper teaches you to have compassion for yourself and for others.

Opal teaches you to be adventurous and fearlessly go for your dreams.

Pink tourmaline encourages emotional healing so you can share love and compassion.

Prehnite facilitates emotional awareness and encourages self-worth.

Pyrite gives you the strength and endurance to face any task.

Red jasper encourages you to believe in yourself and never give up.

Rhodochrosite comforts you with loving and nurturing energies when you're feeling down.

Malachite.

Rhodonite teaches you that sharing love generously is a form of loving yourself.

Rose quartz encourages you to open your heart to love.

Ruby fuchsite reminds you to honour yourself by taking action on your wants and needs.

Rutile empowers you to manifest and achieve your dreams at lightning speed.

Selenite deepens your connection to the divine and purifies your energy and home.

Shungite emanates harmonious centring energy, redirecting feelings of chaos and stress.

Smoky quartz helps you to focus your thoughts, alleviating fears and stress.

Sodalite encourages you to expand your mind beyond mainstream teachings.

Sunstone surrounds you with vibrant energy that fills your whole being with joy.

Tiger's eye reminds you to keep your eye on the prize and move forward without fear.

Turquoise connects you to your wisdom and teaches you to express it with poise.

Unakite releases your bad habits and opens your life to true love.

QUICK
CRYSTAL
AFFIRMATION
GUIDE

Amazonite: I trust myself to make the right choices for me.

Amethyst: I am aligned in spirit, body and mind.

Aquamarine: I allow myself to explore and heal my deepest feelings.

Aventurine: I am deserving of happiness.

Azurite: I am divinely connected to the universe.

Black tourmaline: I am safe.

Bloodstone: I have the courage to move through all of life's challenges.

Blue calcite: I express my feelings, wants and needs with ease.

Blue lace agate: My words hold power, so I choose them wisely.

Carnelian: I am the architect of my reality.

Celestite: I allow myself to rest and feel peace.

Charoite: When I invest in myself I invest in everyone I love.

Citrine: I am a magnet for abundance.

Clear quartz: I amplify my intentions with crystal-clear focus.

Fire agate: I can achieve anything I desire.

Fluorite: I am fearless and focused.

Garnet: I am at peace with where I am.

Hematite: I remain grounded while I integrate my spiritual lessons.

Howlite: I release negativity with every exhale and breathe in positivity.

Iolite: I open my mind to conscious expansion.

Jade: I am happy, healthy and fulfilled.

Kunzite: I give myself permission to heal.

Kyanite: I am the conscious expression of the universe.

Labradorite: I trust my gifts and control where my energy is spent.

Lapis lazuli: I connect to my intuition with ease and express myself authentically.

Larimar: I am powerful when I explore what makes me feel vulnerable.

Lepidolite: I change what I can and accept what I cannot.

Malachite: I am fuelled by the powerful force of love.

Mookaite jasper: My ancestors will guide me when I call to them.

Moonstone: I step into the unknown with courage.

Obsidian: I take ownership for my actions.

Ocean jasper: I am in control of my emotions; my emotions are not in control of me.

Opal: I attract all that I desire with ease and joy.

Pink tourmaline: I open my heart to free-flowing and abundant love.

Prehnite: I love and accept myself for who I am.

Pyrite: My focus and determination are unwavering.

Red jasper.

Red jasper: I believe in myself; I will never give up!

Rhodochrosite: I honour and love myself without reservation.

Rhodonite: I open my heart to others and share my love generously.

Rose quartz: My soul is revived by the powerful force of love.

Ruby fuchsite: I honour myself by prioritising my needs.

Rutile: I am ready to step into my power and towards my destiny.

Selenite: I am protected and purified by divine light frequency.

233

Shungite: I am connected to all of nature's power and potential.

Smoky quartz: My worth is not defined by my productivity.

Sodalite: I open my mind to the mysteries of the universe.

Sunstone: I embrace the radiant light surrounding me.

Tiger's eye: I pounce on opportunities with courage and determination.

Turquoise: I connect to and express my wisdom from lifetimes passed.

Unakite: I open myself to a life of stability and grounded love.

Sunstone.

APPENDIX IV:

QUICK CRYSTAL ELEMENT GUIDE

The *earth* element is associated with health, materialism and stability.

Aventurine	Jade	Prehnite	Shungite
Black tourmaline	Kyanite	Pyrite	Smoky quartz
Bloodstone	Mookaite jasper	Red jasper	Tiger's eye
Clear quartz	Obsidian	Rhodonite	Turquoise
Garnet	Ocean jasper	Rutile	Unakite
Hematite	Opal		

The *air* element is associated with thoughts, intellect and imagination.

Amethyst	Clear quartz	Lapis lazuli	Selenite
Azurite	Howlite	Moonstone	Shungite
Blue calcite	Iolite	Opal	Sodalite
Celestite	Kyanite	Rose quartz	Turquoise
Charoite	Labradorite	Rutile	

Celestite.

The *fire* element is associated with passion, creativity and ambition.

Carnelian	Kyanite	Rhodonite	Tiger's eye
Citrine	Malachite	Rutile	Turquoise
Clear quartz	Opal	Shungite	
Fire agate	Rhodochrosite	Sunstone	

The *water* element is associated with feelings, emotions and intuition.

Amazonite	Fluorite	Lepidolite	Ruby fuchsite
Aquamarine	Kunzite	Opal	Rutile
Aventurine	Kyanite	Pink tourmaline	Shungite
Blue lace agate	Larimar	Prehnite	Turquoise
Clear quartz			

Turquoise.

APPENDIX V:

QUICK CRYSTAL CHAKRA GUIDE

The *crown chakra*, located above the head, governs enlightenment.

Amethyst	Clear quartz	Labradorite	Rutile
Azurite	Howlite	Moonstone	Selenite
Celestite	Kyanite	Opal	Shungite
Charoite			

The *third eye chakra*, located between the brows, governs psychic awareness.

Amethyst	Clear quartz	Lapis lazuli	Rutile
Azurite	Fluorite	Lepidolite	Selenite
Blue calcite	Iolite	Moonstone	Shungite
Celestite	Kyanite	Opal	Sodalite
Charoite	Labradorite		

The *throat chakra*, located in the throat, governs communication.

Amazonite	Clear quartz	Larimar	Rutile
Aquamarine	Kyanite	Ocean jasper	Shungite
Blue calcite	Labradorite	Opal	Turquoise
Blue lace agate	Lapis lazuli		

242

The *heart chakra*, located in the centre of the chest, governs openness to giving and receiving love.

Amazonite	Kyanite	Opal	Rose quartz
Aventurine	Labradorite	Pink tourmaline	Ruby fuchsite
Clear quartz	Lepidolite	Prehnite	Rutile
Fluorite	Malachite	Rhodochrosite	Shungite
Jade	Ocean jasper	Rhodonite	Unakite
Kunzite			

The *solar plexus chakra*, located just above the navel, governs the sense of empowerment.

Charoite	Labradorite	Opal	Rutile
Citrine	Malachite	Prehnite	Shungite
Clear quartz	Mookaite jasper	Pyrite	Sunstone
Fire agate	Ocean jasper	Rhodochrosite	Tiger's eye
Kyanite			

The *sacral chakra*, located just below the navel, governs creative energy.

Carnelian	Kyanite	Opal	Shungite
Citrine	Labradorite	Red jasper	Sunstone
Clear quartz	Mookaite jasper	Rutile	Tiger's eye
Fire agate			

The *root chakra*, located at the base of the spine, governs the sense of stability.

Black tourmaline	Fire agate	Mookaite jasper	Ruby fuchsite
Bloodstone	Garnet	Obsidian	Rutile
Carnelian	Hematite	Opal	Shungite
Citrine	Kyanite	Red jasper	Smoky quartz
Clear quartz	Labradorite	Rhodonite	Tiger's eye

245

QUICK
CRYSTAL
ZODIAC
GUIDE

It's important to realise that your energetic needs are constantly waxing and waning and as such you will always need to work with different stones that are in alignment with the energy you are processing at any given time. However, this quick guide will help you determine which crystals would be ideal for your specific archetype according to the star's placements at the exact moment you were born.

Astrology is full of complexities, but if all you know is your sun's placement then you can use that as a starting point when reading this guide. If you are familiar with your sun, moon and ascending signs, use those three major placements to determine which crystals would be perfect for your unique energy.

ARIES
21 MARCH TO 19 APRIL

Being an Aries means you burn with a fiery passion. You have a determination that makes anything and everything seem possible, reaching for the stars and rarely taking 'No' for an answer. These qualities make you fun, adventurous and successful, and the rest of us wonder where you get all your energy from! In contrast you can be impulsive and unorganised. Your seemingly endless source of energy will eventually deplete and you could burn yourself out if you don't take time to rest.

Crystal recommendation for Aries: FIRE AGATE

Fire agate will keep you grounded while giving you the boost of energy you need to get through your never-ending list of goals. Balancing work and play can be hard, but fire agate will secure your energy firmly in your physical body and will help you to prioritise and re-evaluate what inspires you so you can make time for the things that fulfil you.

TAURUS

20 APRIL TO 20 MAY

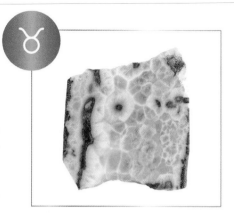

You are practical and organised, and almost everything you do is focused on securing yourself firmly in your comfort zone. You like the finer things in life and are not afraid to work for them. The rest of us wonder how you seem to effortlessly achieve your goals and never seem frazzled but, like the mighty bull, you don't like to be bothered or moved. You can be stubborn and hold a grudge if anyone rubs you the wrong way. You don't have the time or energy for other people's dramas, and while that's understandable you can come across as being cold and unapproachable at times.

Crystal recommendation for Taurus: LARIMAR

Larimar, which is as rare and treasured as you are to your friends and family, has a cooling energy that could calm the mood of even the most stubborn, hangry Taurean. Larimar will soften your heart and allow you to connect with your feelings, forgive more easily and let go of judgement. With the help of larimar you will have a little more patience for others and for yourself.

250

GEMINI
21 MAY TO 20 JUNE

You're a social butterfly with a desire to get the most out of life. You're not afraid to change your mind but that doesn't make you two-faced, as the stereotypes might suggest. You honour your ever-changing feelings and are open to new ideas and experiences, which also means you might become easily bored with things or come across as being unreliable.

Crystal recommendation for Gemini: RUTILATED QUARTZ

Rutilated quartz will amplify all of your best qualities, keeping you inspired, curious and buzzing with energy. In fact, I would recommend you keep it away from you when you're sleeping to avoid a restless night. While you may struggle with reliability at times, rutilated quartz will give you razor-sharp focus so you can follow through on any task. Furthermore, it's a stone of manifesting, so use it to find your higher calling and boredom will be a thing of the past.

CANCER

21 JUNE TO 22 JULY

You easily tune in to the energies of those around you and nurture the people you love. You project strength from the outside, but on the inside you're very sensitive and emotional – more so than people realise. Your sensitivity helps you to understand others, making you a great listener and shoulder to cry on. Be careful you don't spread yourself too thin, because when you overcommit to helping everyone else you leave very little time for yourself. You can't pour from an empty cup.

Crystal recommendation for Cancer: RHODOCHROSITE

Rhodochrosite is all about love and compassion. As a Cancerian you have a tendency to hold on to things, reliving situations over and over again to try to make sense of it in your mind. Rhodochrosite will help you to release emotional blockages and give yourself permission to move on from that pain. Because you feel everything so deeply, it takes you longer to heal. Rhodochrosite offers you the support you need and encourages you to be kind to yourself and make self-care a priority.

LEO

23 JULY TO
22 AUGUST

You're confident, creative and unapologetic and being the centre of attention comes easily to you. Because of this you often steal the limelight. You're a natural leader and come across as being fearless and powerful to the rest of us mere mortals. You're generous, encouraging and loyal to those in your inner circle and have a flair for theatrics, which can be both a good and bad quality depending on your mood.

Crystal recommendation for Leo: CARNELIAN

Carnelian emanates your Leo qualities of courage, confidence, strength and success and resonates perfectly to keep you energised and on the path to empowerment. While you might ordinarily have trouble receiving criticism, carnelian will shift your perspective so that you can embrace this issue and see it as a chance to level up and be a better version of yourself.

VIRGO

23 AUGUST TO
22 SEPTEMBER

Your attention to detail is unparalleled, so much so that you might come across as being a perfectionist. You have a million things on your to-do list and feel as though you have to do them all yourself if you want them done right. You might seem overly critical or intense to some, although you're often more critical of yourself. Try to let the small things go and take a break from worrying every now and then.

Crystal recommendation for Virgo: SMOKY QUARTZ

All of the above might be true of Virgos, but it leaves out an important point: you're an earth sign, and an earth sign needs to connect back to nature to operate at full capacity. Smoky quartz is a stone of practicality that will help you sort out the logistics of your crazy schedule while keeping you grounded and calm. Once you have your schedule organised you can make time for the great outdoors, ideally in a remote place where it's quiet and you can enjoy a bushwalk and listen to the birds.

LIBRA
23 SEPTEMBER TO
22 OCTOBER

Your carefree attitude means you don't like to sweat the small stuff. You thrive in a harmonious and balanced environment and have a lot of love to give, but your accommodating nature puts you at risk of appearing insincere or having others take advantage of you.

Crystal recommendation for Libra: TIGER'S EYE

You need to feel grounded, and tiger's eye can offer you a sense of security. However, you also might need a little help when things aren't going so smoothly and have a tendency to avoid conflict or procrastinate on important issues. Tiger's eye is a stone of strength and independence that is known for its ability to assist in making decisions without being biased or judgemental. This is great for you as a Libran if you struggle with speaking up or making difficult decisions. Tiger's eye will give you the vitality to power through whatever life throws your way so you can get back to being your chilled self.

SCORPIO

23 OCTOBER TO
21 NOVEMBER

You are ambitious and determined in life, which can be intimidating to others who might mistake you as being manipulative or opportunistic. However, they may fail to see that you're also intuitive and highly emotional. When you honour all parts of yourself you'll be in tune with your shadow and can move mountains with sheer willpower. This is a superpower and not something to shy away from.

Crystal recommendation for Scorpio: AQUAMARINE

Aquamarine is known to cool a hot temper, which will come in handy for you as a Scorpio. It also helps with communicating clearly and soothing emotions. Scorpios have a tendency to harbour grudges, but with the help of aquamarine you can lighten your load and let go of situations in which you may be holding on to excessive anger or jealousy.

256

SAGITTARIUS

22 NOVEMBER TO
21 DECEMBER

You're always looking for more, which sets you on the path to great adventures! You have big dreams and are willing to risk it all to attain them. Take time to think things through before you take action, as you may take for granted the wonderful things you already have in your life when you continuously seek something better.

Crystal recommendation for Sagittarius: LAPIS LAZULI

Your thirst for knowledge and understanding of the world is supported by the powerful vibrational frequencies of lapis lazuli, which encourages truthful communication and self-awareness. It opens up your psychic channels so you can see all the possibilities in front of you and the best way to get there. Lapis lazuli will help you to communicate your ideas and thoughts in a way that allows others to understand your grand plans, which would otherwise be outside of their realities.

257

CAPRICORN

22 DECEMBER TO 19 JANUARY

You're successful in everything you put your mind to, and your drive and determination are enviable to the rest of us. You're the loyal friend and confidant everyone else comes to for advice. Being an earth sign means you strive in a stable and organised environment. Be mindful that not everyone else thinks the same way as you: while you think your sarcastic communication is light-hearted, it could come across as being a little harsh to others.

Crystal recommendation for Capricorn: PINK TOURMALINE

Pink tourmaline emanates energies that soothe and nurture. As a Capricorn you place impossibly high standards on yourself, and pink tourmaline will balance your emotions and help you to stay stress free. It will also encourage you to connect with your gentle side, which will help you to be more tolerant and understanding towards others and yourself.

258

AQUARIUS

**20 JANUARY TO
18 FEBRUARY**

You're a forward-thinking eccentric type who is always up for an adventure. Although you also have a strong sense of when it's time to get serious, you can come across as being a bit of a wildcard to others. You're artistic, rebellious and independent, which makes you attractive to others. Be sure to make time for yourself to recharge and process your thoughts.

Crystal recommendation for Aquarius: LABRADORITE

Labradorite is a crystal of transformation and purification that will support your confident nature while insulating you from the energies of those around you. Being such a magnetic and charismatic person, it's important to have a stone that protects you from feeling energetically drained by others. Labradorite is also a great crystal for meditation that will help you unpack your unconscious and explore your inner thoughts.

PISCES

19 FEBRUARY TO 20 MARCH

You're the whimsy daydreamer of your friendship group, and your belief in the magical and impossible inspires those around you. You are naturally intuitive and can pick up on the feelings of others, which can be overwhelming for you as your emotions run deep. Some days you have an incredible ability to express yourself, while on other days you need your alone time. Either way, you harness creativity the rest of us can only dream of. You have a hunger for knowledge but you can sometimes come across as being nosy and oversharing.

Crystal recommendation for Pisces: BLUE LACE AGATE

Blue lace agate will help to realign the energy of your throat chakra and will bring your communication back into balance whether you're expressing too little or too much. Blue lace agate will also calm your emotions and give you confidence and clarity.

ABOUT THE
AUTHOR

Jessica Lahoud is an author and artist and the co-owner of Sydney's iconic crystal shop Mineralism. She was born in Sydney, Australia, and before opening Mineralism spent years studying fine arts at the Sydney College of the Arts and working in live music. She is a third-generation gem and mineral merchant, having grown up in the industry and travelling the world to attend international gem and mineral trade shows. She spends her days offering crystal insights to Australia's spiritual community and continues to travel the world to source crystals for her store.

www.mineralism.com.au

INDEX